To Charlotte & Stu

May God bless!

of you,

Cousin Bill

June 13, 2011

GW00832251

To Live Again

Archeology and History of the Robinson-West
River Plantation 1857-2011

Bill D. West

authorHOUSE®

AuthorHouse™
1663 Liberty Drive
Bloomington, IN 47403
www.authorhouse.com
Phone: 1-800-839-8640

First published by AuthorHouse   3/15/2011

ISBN: 978-1-4567-2102-2 (hc)
ISBN: 978-1-4567-2103-9 (sc)
ISBN: 978-1-4567-2104-6 (e)

Library of Congress Control Number: 2011900281

Printed in the United States of America

This book is printed on acid-free paper.

Certain stock imagery © Thinkstock.

Contents

Chapter 1	Coming Home	1
Chapter 2	Brief History of the Plantation	5
	Era of the Steamboats	6
Chapter 3	Thirty-two Years of Silence	11
Chapter 4	The Awakening	17
Chapter 5	Discoveries and Research	23
	Weapons	24
	Housewares	26
	Tools	27
	Horse and Wagons	28
	Personal Items	31
	Glassware	35
	The Push Broom	35
Chapter 6	State Archeological Site	37
Chapter 7	The First Presentations	41
Chapter 8	The Field Trips	45
Chapter 9	Summer of 2010	53
	San Jacinto County Historical Commission	53
	Application for the State Archeological Landmark	54
	The Old Jail Museum in Coldspring	55
	Topographical Accuracy	55
Chapter 10	A Visit With Bess and Bill Blythe Robinson	57
	Memories	57
	Before 1857?	60
	The Truth-Point Blank	62
	The Well, Wagon Road, Gristmill, and the Dairy	62
	The Slavery Issue	63
	Sam Houston, Governor Wood, and Robert Tod	65

Oakhurst and Snowtown 65
Those Robinson Boys: Major William, Uncle Tod, Robert Tod, Henry, Cornelius, Gilbert, & Young William 68
Letter From Sam Houston to Tod Robinson 70
To Tod Robinson 71
A Family Tradition 72
Henry, and Cornelius Ware Robinson 72
The Honorable Cornelius Ware Robinson 72
Governor Wood's House 73
Gilbert, Eliza Jane, and General Lafayette 74
Young William 76

Chapter 11 Triumph and Tradgedy 79
Tod Sr., Tod Jr. & Mary D 79

Chapter 12 The Last Descendent 85
Elizabeth (Libby) Hansen Robinson 1916-2007 85
State *Historical* Landmark 88

Chapter 13 Jessie Mae Polk (Howard),(1916-) 91
Childhood Friends 91
'Gone With the Wind' 95

Chapter 14 September, 2010 99
'I'm sorry, Aunt Lillie' 99
September 10 In Pursuit of a State **Archeological** Landmark 104
September 11 A Birthday Celebration 105
September 13 Tour & Presentation To The San Jacinto County Historical Commission 106
September 18 Discovery of the 1924 Indian Head Nickel 107
September 22 Discovery of Toy Pistol 107

Chapter 15 Theories 109
The Magneto 109
First Model T in San Jacinto County Recalled 109
The Heart-Shaped Pendant 110

The Blacksmith's Hammer 110
The Double-Edged Axes 111
Padlocks: Sargent, Corbin, & Bohannen 112
Home Comfort Cookstove Shelf 112
Single Shot Shotgun 112
The Toy Pistol 113
Dover 'Sad' Iron 113
1847 Rogers Bros. Silver Spoon 114

Chapter 16 Interview With Thomas Earl and Jeanne Walters 117
First Black Co-ed at Rice University 120
First 'Federal' Post Office Building in Point Blank 121

Chapter 17 Billie Trapp—Educator, Historian 127
October 7, 2010 127
Letters From Mary D. 130
The Grey Goose' 133
Swartout 134
The Gindrats 134
Point Blank Stores 135
Governor Wood and Chief 'Ben Ash' 135
A Tribute to Billie 136
Harry, Ora Lee, and Tod, Sr. 136
'A Bear in the Woods?' 137
Importance of A State **Archeological** Landmark 139

Chapter 18 Becoming A State Archeological Landmark 141
October, 2010 141

Resources 147

The Robinsons

1.   Tod Robinson--1812-1870
2.   Major William Robinson--1799-1882
3.   Robert Tod Robinson--1826-1878
4.   Henry Ware Robinson--1828-1897
5.   Gilbert Du Motier Robinson----------------------------------1834-1885
6.   Tod, Sr. Robinson---1856-1927
7.   Cornelius Ware Robinson--------------------------------------1863-1926
8.   Tod Jr. (Little Tod) Robinson--------------------------------1885-1931
9.   Aubrey Hugh Robinson--1891-1945
10. Bess Blythe Tyson Robinson----------------------------------1914-
11. Libby Hansen Robinson--1916-2007
12. Hugh Tod Robinson--1920-1936

Chapter 1

Coming Home

The deep snow and raging waters of Oak Creek Canyon in northern Arizona had finally sent us packing to return home to our beloved east Texas. It was 1978, and my days in Arizona as an educator, coach, and United States forest ranger were over. Sedona was beautiful, but home was Texas, so my wife Barbara, and I, and four little ones embarked on the 1200 mile journey, driving two U-haul trucks, day and night. There was never any doubt, after an absence of twenty years, we would find our new home in the sweet fragrance of the piney woods. Childhood memories of hunting and fishing in the thickets and along the rivers ran rampant in my reminiscent mind as we rolled on down the highway. Our families were buried there, and there would be our final resting place.

Selling our house in beautiful Oak Creek gave us a little nest egg so that we could begin the search for a new home. We wanted something traditional and out in the country. The long hours of coaching had prompted us to live life at a slower pace. Albeit, employment would come in the form of continuing to teach Physical Education and History in Coldspring, Texas. After securing a job, the search for a home began.

"I know, I'll take a short cut to Coldspring on State Highway 156. It's a country road and there won't be much traffic. Besides, it parallels Lake Livingston. I hear it's a scenic drive." Within a few miles of Coldspring on 156 in Point Blank, I glanced to my right and there it was---a stately looking two story southern style home quietly hidden behind lazy oak trees and facing the Trinity River. It was for sale. The gate was locked, so I parked and walked up to the peaceful setting. The home sat on a hill with an over grown pasture in the front, and thick woods all around. Long veils of Spanish moss hung from towering oaks everywhere. It appeared lonely and abandoned, and yet it stood proud as though it needed no one to speak of its value. There was an eerie silence as I approached the large columns supporting the structure. Somehow I had the strange feeling that I was walking on hallowed ground, and the eyes of the Victorian home were watching my every step. A Texas historical marker proclaimed a history which dated back to 1857. It read 'The Robert Tod Robinson House,' and explained that it was once a cotton plantation. "Interesting," I thought. I sat down on the front porch steps, layed back, and enjoyed the warm Texas sun which I had not known since my high school days. I thought," Will this be our home? Will this be where I choose to continue raising my family? No, it's too expensive. Not on a school teacher's salary. But, maybe if I talk to the owner..." The Texas senate was in session in Austin, and Bill Blythe (Robinson), who was a state representative was obligated to his duties. He also represented the family for sale of the plantation. We would have to wait. Lucky for us, the Robinsons preferred a young couple with children to buy the estate. They knew the plantation was virtually dead, and hoped the laughter of little children would liven up the estate once again. When Bill returned from Austin, it took a month of negotiations with several members of the Robinson family to conclude the deal. I didn't realize it at the time, but when I placed my signature on the final papers, 120 years of blood, sweat, tears, joy, and happiness for the Robinson family came to an end on this plantation. The place was ours. I called my mother in Arizona, and told her that we had bought a place in Point Blank, located in east Texas. She replied, 'Oh no, not in Point Blank. People there live very poorly, and everyone lives in the country. Don't you remember going there as a child to visit your Aunt Lillie and Uncle Ivan Jones in their two room log house? Remember how Aunt Lillie struggled to put a decent meal on the table. She had to kill a chicken and gather a few peas out of the garden. Don't you remember taking a bath in a No. 3 washtub after drawing water from a well? Son, I raised you to be educated, and now you want to go right back to your country roots." It was bad enough that I had taken her grandchildren away from her, so I reassured her that things had changed in deep east Texas, and now maybe I could help bring education to these little Texans. Yet, when I toured the local country roads, I saw three things which reminded me of those youthful days of the past---an occasional outhouse, a deep well where water was still drawn by bucket and pulley, and an old fella still plowing his field with a mule. I also looked for the log house, and found that it was still there.

Plantation House

When we moved into the plantation house, we had to battle our way. The old house was infested with hornets, and roaches, and rats, and spiders, and a few other critters. The electrical system was the original and scary to look at, and the plumbing was the old galvanized pipe, and difficult to repair. Also, the foundation of sandstone pillars were starting to crumble. There was an old carbide plant buried and rusting in the back yard, which had provided for gas lights in the house. The once proud and historic home stood ailing, sick, and lonely, hurting for repair and desperate for the return of the laughter of children and family. But we were young, proud to have what we had bought, and looking forward to the task. I looked square in the eye of my new found friend, the old house, and whispered, "Don't worry, Tara will rise again."

Bill and Barbara West
2009

Chapter 2

Brief History of the Plantation

The magnitude of what we had bought did not set in until one day when I picked up an article written in 1975 by the late Colonel William Jackson Blythe, husband of Bess Robinson, and father of Bill Blythe. Paraphrasing the article, it read:

Robinson Plantation, 1846
   ''Major William Robinson, in 1846, was accompanied by his three eldest sons, Robert Tod, Henry, and Gilbert from Alabama, to Texas where they searched along the Trinity and Brazos rivers for suitable land relatively close to the port of Galveston, where they expected to produce, sell, and ship cotton to Europe. The sons Uncle Tod also made the trip. Uncle Tod settled in Brazoria County where he established a newspaper and was elected to the Congress of the Republic of Texas for three terms. Major Robinson, on the other hand, purchased over 3500 acres of land in San Jacinto and Polk Counties, and returned to Alabama to his wife, Eliza Jane, leaving the sons to settle in Texas. In 1857, a man who owned slaves was hired to build the two story house which stands today.
   Robert Tod was named executor in his father's will, and in 1879, gained control of the plantation. He married Mary Louise McGowen, and they had six children: Tod, William,

Fannie, Harry, Lee, and Hill. Robert Tod, held the lands only five months before passing it on to his son, Tod.

Tod Robinson, known as Tod, Sr., further increased and developed the land, producing cotton, engaging in the mercantile and banking business, and operating a cotton gin. He also became the first Post Master in Point Blank (Pointe Blanche) from 1884-1914, a position held until 1949 by his daughter, Ruby Lee Harwood. Rudolph C. Hansen, who married Tod Robinson's grandaughter, Ora Elizabeth Robinson, served as Post Master 1953-1966.

Tod Robinson's application for a Post Office asked that it be named Point Blanc. The Postal records show that someone drew a line through the requested name, and substituted Point Blank.

Children born to Tod and his wife, Ora Lee (McClanahan), were Ruby Lee, Fannie Rose, Aubrey Hugh, and Robert Tod, Jr. By a previous marriage to Lizzie Henry, Tod had a daughter Bessie Robinson (Adams).

Descendents of Major Robinson now living, or holding property in San Jacinto County are Elizabeth Hansen, daughter of Hugh Robinson, Elizabeth Henderson, daughter of Robert Tod, Jr., Bessie Lee Tyson Blythe, and Thomas Brown Tyson, Jr. , children of Fannie Rose Robinson and Thomas Brown Tyson. William Jackson Blythe, Jr., son of Bessie Lee Tyson Blythe, and her husband Col. William Jackson Blythe, Sr.... ''

A French governess, and friend of the family, Florence Dissosway, came from Alabama at the Major's request, to educate the Robinson grandchildren. She came in on the steamboat, 'Early Bird,' and when she approached the plantation from around the bend on the Trinity River, all she could see was white (cotton). She called it the 'Pointe Blanche,' French for white point. The name was adopted by the local people, and evolved into the name Point Blank.

Era of the Steamboats

No discussion of the early Robinson plantation would be complete without mentioning the most important mode of transportation and travel, the era of the steamboats. Via the steamboat, the Robinsons could order and ship their goods, visit other plantations up and down the Trinity, boy could meet girl, and they could travel to Houston. In the book, <u>San Jacinto County: A glimpse into the past,</u> an article written by the late Iva Blalock explained the era of the <u>Steamboats on the Trinity River:</u>

The Trinity River flows down from Fort Worth, Texas, and winds its unhurried way through the outskirts of Point Blank, ending its journey in the busy waters of the gulf of Mexico. From the beginning of the settlement of Texas until the middle 1870s, the Trinity River served as a means of transportation. Steamboats on their way to and from coastal ports, made regular stops a Drews Landing, Cedar Landing, Swartout, Johnson's Bluff, Patricks Ferry, Geneva, Jones Bluff, Velco, and other ports. They carried loads of cotton, hides, wood, and lumber to market, returning with passengers, bolts of cloth, barrels of whiskey, flour, salt, coffee, and other supplies.

It has been said there are 98 steamboats known to have operated on the Trinity River between 1835 and 1875. Some of the steamboats were the Black Cloud, Branch T. Archer, Ruthven, Early Bird, Graham, Colonel D. S. Gage, Trinity, Brazos, Kate, Ida Reese, Bell of Texas, Correro, Neptune, Scioto Bell, Friend, Mary Clifton, Nora, Wanderer, C. B. Lee, Vesta, Pioneer, Ellen Franklin, Wren, Indianna, Molly Hamilton, and many more. "Drummers" came by steamboat to take orders for goods.

There is no one living who knows what year the steamboats started running on the Trinity River. However, some of the old timers remembered their forefathers saying it was the early 1800s.

In 1834, Isaac Jones, (one of my relatives), and family, came from Vicksburg, Mississippi, and settled on the Trinity River bank. He received a league of Mexican Land Grant on the west side of the river near Point Blank. In 1858, Isaac had a port and a ferry called Jones Bluff. Steamboats made regular stops at the port.

George T. Wood (1795-1858), who became the second Governor of Texas in 1847, chartered a boat in 1839 at Georgia, and moved his family with thirty slaves to Houston, where he studied law and passed the bar. His wife brought some mulberry bushes and silkworms. Later, Woods bought a plantation on the west bank of the Trinity River near Point Blank. Mrs. Wood had her Mulberry bushes planted and the bushes grew. She made her own silk, and sold some of the cloth for ten dollars per yard. The Woods established a boat landing, and when a steamboat whistle was heard, night or day, the whole houshold hurried to enjoy the excitement an arriving boat created. One night the steamboat, James Jenkins, and the Captain asked for Mrs. Wood. He gave her a Bible, an heirloom she left in Georgia, that had been sent to her. Sometimes, a steamboat Captain would invite the Wood children, and children of the slaves, for a cruise up the river. The children would walk back home over the rough, sandy land road.

Governor George Tyler Wood
1795-1858

In 1858, Mary Wood, daughter of George and Mrs. Wood, went to Galveston and returned on the luxurious Bayou City steamboat.

This writer's grandfather, Alfred Aden, came from Kentucky to Anauac by boat and caught a steamboat there, and arrived at the port of Swartout in 1849. He boarded at the John Victory home. Mr Victory was a farmer with a large plantation and slaves. Alfred taught school in the church-school at Swartout. It was here that he met Mary Cochran and they married in 1851.

After many years, the sandy banks of the Trinity River began to crumble, carrying trees and sand into the river. The river changed its course in several places, widening its banks. Water was lowered causing steamboats to hit snags and sandbars. Many steamboats were sunk. At flood times, the river could be navigated, but dangerously and with great skill.

Governor George T. Wood shipped a load of cotton to Galveston on a steamboat. The boat hit a snag in the river and went down, losing the cotton and the crew. It was a big loss for Governor Wood, for the bales of cotton were not insured.

Jeff McGrew, who was 100 years old in 1967, told this writer of a tragedy on the river. 'I was too young to work in the field and too small to stay at home by myself," said Jeff. So Pa took me to the blacksmith shop with him. The shop belonged to a white man, but Pa did most of the work. He sharpened plows and saws, made sweep stocks, and repaired wagons for farmers. The blacksmith shop stood near the bank of the river, and when a steamboat came along, everyone would run out to wave at the crew. One day we heard a whistle blow on a boat. "That's the White Cloud coming," Pa said, laying his tools down. "Let's go watch it." "Just as the White Cloud got in sight of us, it hit a sandbar,"said Jeff. The boat went down, carrying the crew, passingers, and freight with her. It was a long time before I watched a steamboat pass by again," said Jeff, sadly.

Ben Caswell, whose mother died when he was small remembered his father taking him on horseback to load wood on a steamboat. "Pa made me sit on the bank while he and W. C. Knight loaded the wood onto the boat," said Ben, smiling. "Years later, Pa told me the Captain had to wait until the water rose in the river before taking off."

Dick Blalock and Jimmie Jones were buffalo fishermen. They would go to the river in a wagon and camp several days. Buffalo fish sucked the bait and they had to fish on the bottom of the river. In 1905, while fishing at the Dan Barnett place, they brought back a piece of iron that came from a sunken steamboat. The Blalocks used the iron for a stepping block, for a woman to get on a side saddle.

The Geeslin family lived at Stephen Creek near the Trinity River. When Stella Geeslin Horton was a girl, steamboats no longer traveled the river. The water was low and she and her brother and friends swam in the river. "Sometimes we could see part of a sunken steamboat," said Stella. "We would swim out and play on the part that stood up out of the water."

It has been many years since steamboats have traveled on the Trinity

River. In 1969, Lake Livingston dam was built. Locks were installed at Camilla, Texas, causing the river to rise to its river bank, and backwater stretching out for miles. Today, in 1987, the only boats that can be seen are sailboats, and fishermen in small boats cruising up and down the Trinity River.

Chapter 3

Thirty-two Years of Silence

We had bought more than just a house in the country in 1978. We had bought a piece of Texas history. The last living descendent of the Robinson family, who lived in this house had moved to a new location in Point Blank five years earlier. After the loss of her husband, Libby could no longer take care of such a large estate, and they had no children to inherit the plantation. It had to be sold.

In a taped interview years later, Libby shared with us more details of her life on the plantation. Cotton was grown in large quantities, shipped on steamboats down the river and sold in Europe. Libby was born in the living room and grew up on the estate. She remembered as a little girl intentionally sitting on the front porch just to listen to the folks singing who were picking cotton close to the house. The plantation had been in the Robinson family since it was built by slave labor in 1857. In their family had been soldiers, statesmen, and civic leaders throughout the past 120 years. Even the town of Point Blank had derived its name from the Robinson plantation. We would be the first family outside of the Robinsons to own this estate.

As the years began to pass, we did all the things that families in the country tend to do. In the 80's we had gardens and chickens, and cows and horses. We had family reunions and ball games. The girls would provide home entertainment by singing, dancing, and putting on one-act plays in the living room.

Occasionally, we would mention the history of the house to our visitors. We would tell them that 'we sleep in the same bedroom where General Sam Houston once slept.' To us, this tale was not only possible, but probable. The Robinsons said that sometimes you could hear the floors creak at night. 'It is the General walking the floor worrying about the future of Texas.' At reunions and other gatherings we would casually comment that ' The ol' place has lots of history behind it,' and that's about all we would say. I hadn't heard any boards creaking, and I certainly was not superstitious . Yet, there were times when I would stare at the old Greek revival home out of respect, and it seemed to convey the thought to me that it had much more to say about its illustrious history, but I chose to ignore these feelings, and get on with the busy life we led. We were too involved with farm, family, and ball games. At times, things got rough financially though, and we even thought about selling the old place. It was the monster of maintenance and upkeep. But since the discovery of the artifacts, my lovely daughter Gina , who never wanted to sell the plantation in the first place, reminded me, ''Dad, just look at what you would have never known and discovered if you had sold our home.''

The time came , however, when the once abandoned estate needed a name to represent its history, its purpose, and its new family, the Wests. 'Our family gathered, and decided it would be named 'The West River Plantation' for as long as we owned it.

The summer days were hot and the winters were very cold. You see, we had overlooked one small thing when we bought the house. There was no central air or heat. We could heat the living room and the kitchen with a wood stove, but that was the extent of our warmth. We could not afford propane gas. In the summers at night we would lie in bed with the big windows open, and sweat as we listened to the coyotes, the bullfrogs, and the hoot owls. How in the world did the Robinsons put up with this? For sure, they were tough. They also had ways to survive that we have never known. Our company and relatives would not stay with us, and we couldn't blame them. After ten years of burning up and freezing inside the house, we invested in central air and heat. This would forever change the environment inside the house. No longer would we reach into the closet and have to wear humidified mildewed clothes, and the relatives and visitors actually began to spend the night.

Our son and three daughters, Vince, Leah, Gina, and Julie graduated from the local high school, and within a few years were married. We had always placed strong emphasis on family. One of the daughters, Leah, said,

'Dad, I want an all Southern wedding. I want to be married on our front porch. I want the groomsmen to wear top hats and canes, white gloves, and the long tailed tuxedos. I want the bridesmaids to wear southern belle dresses complete with wide brimmed hats and parasols. You know, just like in *Gone With the Wind*. I also want two horse drawn carriages with surrey fringe to bring the wedding party up from the highway.' And so it was, just as she asked. Though born in Arizona, she made a beautiful, blonde, Southern belle bride. It was a storybook wedding. There were many guests, and people stopped along the highway to witness this page of antebellum history. During all the celebration, once again I would stare at the old house, and get the feeling that this was not the first time for such a glorius wedding on this plantation.

Leah's Wedding
1985

In the late 1980s the grandchildren began to show up. By the mid 90s, we had eleven little gifts from God. There were nine boys, and two girls. By the turn of the century, our talented grandchildren were performing on the front porch at celebrations like the Fourth of July. There was Kevin on the drums, Brian and Eric on the guitars, John, Brandon, Shannon, and Kelly doing the singing, Justin and Joey doing one-act plays, while Laura and Brett hosted as the MCs. The West family was rockin' and rollin.' I could swear that I saw the columns on the old house bend a knee a couple of times, and smile.

As the grandchildren began to grow, they were naturally curious about the history of Grandma & Grandpas house. As I would attempt to briefly explain some of its past, I always had the feeling within that there was much more history here than I was aware of, and this house of antiquity, which I had a great affection for, was trying to tell me so.

1899 Five Cent Piece

Gold Ring
John R. Woods and Son 1850

There were a few inspiring moments in the 80s & 90s which hinted that the land held secrets of history unimaginable to me. But we never took the hint. There was the time in 1985 when I was digging in the flower bed in the front yard for weeds, not for artifacts. Suddenly, there was a coin. After washing it off at the water faucet, it turned out to be an 1899 Miss Liberty five cent piece. I glanced back at the house, and it seemed to smile. They were called five-cent pieces because this was before they were made from the alloy nickel. I never really thought to ask myself 'who dropped this coin, and what were the conditions here in 1899?' I was excited about finding it though, so I took it to the jewelers in Huntsville. I had them to dip this piece of history in gold, put a chain band around it, and make a necklace out of it. I gave the necklace to Barbara for our anniversary. But I never took the hint that maybe there was more. Ten years passed and another whispering hint came along. Barbara was hoeing the weeds in her garden one July day in 1995 when she looked down and caught a glimpse of gold. When she picked it up, it appeared to be a broken band, possibly a ring. We took it inside, washed it off, and there appeared the initials 'WMA', along with the gold trademark 'W'. It was definitely someone's gold ring. We took the broken band to the jeweler in Huntsville and asked if they could repair the ring. She said, 'Yes we can.' In a couple of weeks I returned for the ring. It looked brand new. Once again, it shined with the warm glow of solid gold. We were never able to establish the identity of the initials, but the gold 'W' trademark indicated the ring was made by John R. Woods & Son jewelers, New York City, 1850. Again, a gold chain with the ring made a nice necklace for Barbara, and a conversation piece.

Before we knew it, thirty-two years had passed since buying the estate. During that time, mostly through the efforts of our son, Vince, we gradually cleared the land which mother nature had so thoroughly reclaimed. We needed more pasture, for animals and hay. As we unveiled the landscape, we were awed at the natural beauty of rolling hills and valleys, sprinkled with ponds, and bordering a wilderness creek. The Robinson's knew what they were doing when they selected this, the prettiest part of God's green earth in Texas. By 2009, we had cleared most of the land. Behind the house, however, the acreage was still thickly wooded. In fact, when we bought the home 32 years earlier, the land lay virtually undisturbed since the plantation days. The summer of 09 brought the necessity to clear more land for grazing, so the thicket behind the house was cleared with a bulldozer. As a result, the voices of silence would begin to speak and the Robinson Plantation would suddenly begin to live again.

Chapter 4

The Awakening

The first cool breeze of September in 2009 inspired Barbara to stroll by the pond early on a Sunday morning. The cattails swayed in the breeze and a family of ducks were getting ready to ride with the wind. She was talking on the cell phone to Julie, or Toughy, as we call her, the youngest of our four. As she walked toward a restful bench, Barbara had a serendipitous encounter. She glanced down and thought she saw an embedded coin. She picked it up and started brushing it off. She saw part of a date, "Hmm, 58, I remember that year, 1958. I was 17." Then she brushed it off again. It wasn't 1958, it was 1858. " Excuse me, Julie," Barbara said, " I just found a coin dated 1858. It appears to be a silver half-dollar." Julie shouted on the other end, "Mom, if it's worth any money, I get half, because you were talking to me when you found it."

The coin was a seated Miss Liberty silver half-dollar. It was heavily coated with dirt and corrosion. At first, we couldn't decide what to do with it, whether to clean it up, try to sell it or whatever. We checked on the internet for value of a coin like this. In mint condition, they sold for as much as $400.00 We began to realize, though, that the value of this coin was greatest in its relation to the history of this place. We could never sell it. It had to stay right here where it was found. The experts on the internet advised us to leave the coin as it was found. But we felt that if you can't see its beauty, what is it good for? Barb scrubbed it with polish until it shined once more with the radiant beauty of silver. It became her pride and joy. One day, when she wasn't looking, I took the coin to a trophy store in Huntsville and asked them to display it in a beautiful desk set. They inlaid the coin into decorative glass and cut the history of the coin in the glass. It read:

> This coin was found on the West River Plantation by Barbara West on September 20, 2009, in Point Blank, Texas. It is likely the first time it has been touched by human hands in 152 years. The last person to hold this coin was probably Robert Tod Robinson, who established this plantation in 1857. In 1858, James Buchannen was President (just before Lincoln), the Civil War had not yet begun, Texas had just become a state, and the Indians still lived on their lands in the West." It has thirteen stars on it, and is called the seated Miss Liberty half-dollar. On the tail side is the eagle with a flag on his breast, and arrows and branches in the talons. The letter O is below the talons, indicating the coin was minted in New Orleans. It is said to be one of the rarest of the silver half-dollars.

1858 Silver Half Dollar

This was my gift to her. A few days later in early October, my son Vince, and I were walking across the newly cleared land behind the house.

Suddenly, I stumbled on a piece of iron jutting out of the ground. "What is this, son," I asked. It's shaped kind of funny, but what is it?," I continued. Vince, excellent horseman that he is, answered, "Dad, that's a saddle horn!" It was the iron horn which is placed on a saddle frame before the leather is applied. The rest of the saddle must have disentegrated in the ground. It had to be very old. And then it struck me! **What is going on here, I thought."** First, the coin, now this horn, the gold ring, and the 1899 coin from years past. Look closer at the ground: broken glass, bits of metal. I glanced at my old friend, the plantation house, "Is this what you've been trying to tell me, that there is more, maybe much more buried here? No, the house is not trying to tell me anything. I am not superstitious. Yet, it would make sense. A large plantation, lots of workers, a big operation, the ground undisturbed, 120 years all point toward more artifacts buried in this ground." On the same day, I took the saddle horn to a saddle expert in the little town of Onalaska. I asked, "Do you have any idea how old this horn is, or anything about it?" The old cowboy studied the horn carefully. "I think what you have here is possibly a saddle from the mid 1800s, probably the Civil War era. I have seen these before." My only thought was,"I need to buy a metal detector."

1858 Coin gift to Barbara
2010

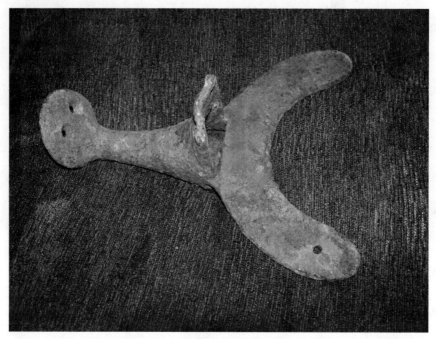

Saddle horn

Craigslist provided the means to buy a quality metal detector for a reasonable amount of cash. It was fun learning to use it. When you get close to an object, it beeps. When you get right above an object, the detector rings like a bell. Sometimes it lies though. When it reads as a coin, it often turns out to be a nail. The entire family, including the grandkids, began to search in earnest. Mid October would bring the first intended discoveries.

In the same area where we found the saddle horn, we began to find housewares, tools, farm implements, and weapons. Finding very old bottles were a bonus. They often were buried with the metal. In the evenings, our family would sit around the table and make up stories and possible truths about the things we had found. For example, we just knew that saddle horn we found belonged to Robert Tod, and the saddle was probably a gift from the General himself, Sam Houston. We began to find so many items(around 50), that by December, I began to feel a strong sense of responsibility toward their preservation. I thought, "Hey, wait just a minute, you need to do something toward preserving these artifacts. You can't just leave them lying around with no record and no intended purpose. You are, after all, an educator."

The top of our two story barn had been a recreation room for the grandchildren for the past several years, but they seldom used it anymore.

It was perfect. We could put the artifacts on display up there. They would be undisturbed, and anyone could visit and see them. We could convert it into a museum. We would build a museum. My daughter, Leah, grandson John, and I went to work building cabinets around the walls, complete with glass tops, red background cloth, and lights. We hung signs for categories such as farm implements, glassware, etc. We provided a table with history and information about the plantation on it. We hung flags which once represented Texas. In addition, Trey Cook, my brother-in-law, donated several glass cases for display. For the first time, things finally made sense. The land and home we had bought was rich in Texas history, and now we were going to have an opportunity to share it with others. The waking of the artifacts would breathe life into the plantation once again.

The "Museum"

Chapter 5

Discoveries and Research

As a Forest Ranger in Arizona, part of my duties were to help preserve and protect the artifacts and ruins of the Anasazi and Hohokam Indian civilizations. This experience gave me the mind set for preservation. The conscience to document the discoveries we were making came in the form of a thick notebook, and photography. In the notebook, I began to number the items with the following information: item description, date it was found, who found it, how deep the item was buried, and it's distance & direction from a point of reference. There was a power pole in the middle of the area where we were finding most of the artifacts. This pole became the point of reference, or in archeological terms, the 'datum point.' I also created a chart to illustrate visually the discovery location of each item. You could look at the chart and see where everything had been found. It wasn't 100% pinpoint accurate, but it was better than three cowpies from an oak tree. I took photos of each item and included them in the beginnings of a slide show, which could be burned onto a DVD. Eventually, I developed the following procedure when discovering an artifact:

1. Find artifact
2. Record location & depth
3. Record on chart
4. Clean up for possible words or designs
5. Take photo, enter into slide show
6. Place in museum with research

The fall and winter months brought our children, grandchildren, and other realatives, especially during the Christmas holidays, and all wanted to dig. I insisted though, that either me or my son, Vince, be present, so that proper procedure would be followed.

Early on one frosty morning, grandson John got a signal and started digging. Deeper and deeper he dug. At eight inches down he struck silver, that is, a silver plated spoon. There were words on the back of the handle. It read, "H. Sears & Son, 1865." My first thoughts were, "Wow, the last year of the war. I wonder who was the last person to enjoy a meal with this spoon. Was it in joy and celebration, or was it in fear and sorrow? One thing for sure, we were in a location where a house once stood. Earlier in September, Vince had also discovered a small table- ware spoon, which read, "Rogers nickel silver-1847. It was buried nine inches deep. We learned that objects buried 8 to 10 inches deep date to the very first days of the plantation, 150 years ago. Every time we made a find, we looked for words or designs, some way to identify its origin and age. I believe the Lord has waited for the invention of the internet to allow us to find these artifacts. With any clue at all, we could go to the internet and find valuable information. Also, neighbors and friends helped us to identify some of the unknown items.Many artifacts were damaged or broken, or were parts off of a larger object like a clevis off of a plow. I found that the artifacts were much more meaningful if I placed a photo with it to illustrate its purpose. A picture is certainly worth a thousand words. Below are listed some of the artifacts we have found, and the interesting research that came with them:

Weapons

1. <u>Double-barreled shotgun:</u> twin barrels, heavily encrusted, buried ten inches deep. Est. 1857. Used for hunting small game to put food on the table.
2. <u>Single shot shotgun:</u> Design indicates maker is Harrington & Richardson Firearms, 1871.

Single shot shotgun
Herrington and Richardson Firearms, 1871

3. <u>Shotgun shells:</u> Writing on the shells read "UMC, New Club, 12 guage." Research showed that UMC stood for Union Metallic Cartridge Co., mid to late 1800s. UMC became Remington.

4. <u>Derringer:</u> Remington type 3, .41rimfire, 1912. Only the handle is left.

5. <u>Pistol:</u> Volcanic .22, blank, made in Italy, 1950's.

6. <u>Two Pocket knives:</u> buried six inches deep. Est. 1900.

7. <u>Sterling silver pocket knife siding:</u> The heads of four hunting dogs are carved into the side of this treasure. Est. 1857.

Sterling Silver Pocket Knife Siding

Housewares

Housewares came in many forms and reflected the toughness, strength, and resilience of both the early pioneer men and women. There were stove parts, bed frames, scissors, sewing machine pulleys, silverware, jar lids, clothing irons, and buttons.

1. W<u>ood burning stoves:</u> for cooking and staying warm. Parts of these stoves were found, such as doors, vents, hot plates, and shelves.

2. <u>A fancy shelf or rack </u>was found, and at first we had no idea what it was off of. It had an HC in the middle of it, with flower décor on either side of the letters. I noticed that the flowers were identical to the symbol on the side of the New Orleans Saints football helmets. I had a teacher friend at work who was a big Saints fan, and had the nickname 'Moose.' So, I asked him, "Hey Moose, what is that funny looking symbol called on the side of the Saints helmet?" He said, "That's a fleur de Lis, French for flower of spring." I went straight to my computer, and suspecting that the rack might be part of

a wood cookstove, I typed in 'antique fleur de lis woodstove.' A picture of a wood cookstove flashed on the screen. The HC stood for Home Comfort, the style was fleur de lis, made in 1864. The rack we found was a shelf attached to the side of the stove. It's purpose was to set those hot pans of oatmeal on to cool off. The shelf also had a bar on it, used for a towel rack.

3. <u>Two Clothing irons-</u> Pioneer men had to step lightly around pioneer women. These ladies of the South were very strong. The clothing irons they used weighed five plus pounds, and they would iron for hours.

4. 'Sad iron'-This dainty little clothing iron, found by my daughter-in-law, Karla, had words on it, but barely distinguishable. It appeared to read, 'Rover bad iron'. So I typed on the internet the same words. But the internet asked, "Did you mean 'Dover Sad Iron?' I responded with a quick 'yes.' Next, a picture appeared of a little iron, identical to the one we found. The iron in the picture was 2x4 inches, and had a cover with a handle which fit over the iron. It's purpose was to iron the lace on young ladies dresses. It was made in 1900.

5. <u>Boyd's Genuine Porcelain Lined Cap</u>—These milk white inserts were made beginning in the late 1800s to resolve the problem of metal and rust from the cap getting into the canned food.

Tools

The tools that we have found suggests a life of backbreaking work, a spirit for surviving, cooperative sharing, sacrifice, and close family togetherness. There were axes, hatchets, splitting wedges, blacksmiths hammer, padlocks, square nails, and files.

1. <u>W. Bohannen padlock:</u> This was an exciting find: A padlock made of solid brass and in excellent condition. It still had a short chain attached to it, and was heavily encrusted with dirt and grime. When freed from its dark dungeon below the ground, I took it immediately to the steel brush grinding wheel, hoping it would have a message for me. A few minutes on the wheel, and there were the words, "W. (Wilson) Bohannen, Brooklyn, New York, Pat. Date May 26, 1885. This padlock could have been used to secure the Robinson's personal property, or it could have been used at the switch on a railroad track. It's

condition suggests that if a key could be made for it, the lock would probably work.

Other heavy padlocks were found: Sargent & Co., 1860, and Corbin Lock Co-1882.

2. <u>Plow wrench-</u>Flat, open ended, and buried 8" deep, this wrench had writing on the side. Even after cleaning, the letters were barely distinguishable. As I turned it in the sun at a slanted angle, I thought I could see the name,'B F Avery.' I went to the internet and typed in 'antique avery wrench.' The result was the Benjamin Franklin Avery & Sons Company, Louisville, Kentucky, 1865. He was a maker of plows and plow wrenches.

3. <u>Three Double-edged axes:</u> The plantation house is made of solid logs. These logs were covered with the present day siding in 1919. However, one can look under the house and see the huge timbers (one foot square) all the way across, which make up the foundation. They are made of cypress and were hewed out with axes, and notched together. You can still see the axe marks. The axes we found, because they were buried ten inches deep, could have been the same axes used to build this two-story structure.

4. <u>Blacksmiths hammer:</u> The Robinsons could not run down to Tractor Supply, or to the local hardware store, or even to the town blacksmith, because there wasn't any. All of their iron works had to be done by their own blacksmith. The blacksmith hammer we found, as well as a homemade spur, and other artifacts testify to this.

5. <u>Cotton hoes:</u> The one tool, more than any other, which most represents plantation life, is the cotton hoe. We have found more cotton hoes than any other single artifact. This hoe is different from modern hoes. It is bigger, heavier, and wider, and the handle slips through a large hole at the top of the hoe. Use this hoe all day, and you get a better workout than if you had gone to the gym.

Horse and Wagons

We have found more items from the horse and buggy days than from any other era. The plantation is living again. Now we can see and touch the very same objects that were the core of peoples lives so long ago, and, if you listen close enough, you can almost hear them speaking, thanking us for bringing them up from the dark and dismal world of the dead. We have found riding bits, snaffle bits, half-cheek snaffle bits, cow and oxen bells, wagon seat springs, wagon wheel hub rings, axle sleeves, doubletrees, singletrees, and a homemade cowboy's spur.

1. Silver plated buffalo head horse bit: It's 1860, and you just received in the steamboat mail from back East, a beautiful, shiney new, silver plated bit with a buffalo head on either side. Your fancy bridle and saddle is an added compliment to this expensive bit. You can't wait to dress up your finest steed in this regalia. So must the Robinsons have felt when this silver horse's bit arrived. We found it ten inches deep in the ground in a different location than most of the items. Maybe it was a special place. We also found a small horseshoe, which would fit an Arabian. Maybe this was the special horse, or the shoe could have fit a mule, which also has small feet. Other than the buffalo bit, we found three other riding bits, and several other snaffle, and half-cheek snaffle bits.

Silver plated
bridle bit
Late 1800s

2. Double trees: The metal from two doubletrees were brought to me by my son, Vince, both dug up near the datum pole. Neither of us had any idea what we were holding in our hands.

They resembled shackles, which I thought a possibility. More than likely, I felt they had something to do with horses and wagons. They laid around the house for a few days, when I thought about taking them to a long time black friend of mine, Arthur Gene, who worked at the county landfill. I needed to make a trip there anyway, so I took the artifacts with me. Arthur had been around horses all his life, so I thought maybe he had a clue. "Hey, Arthur, do you have any idea what these are,?" I asked. He replied, "Yes sir, Mr. West, That's them doubletrees. Man, those are really old." "I hate to show my ignorance, Arthur, but what the heck are doubletrees?," I continued. Arthur explained, "That's what hitches the horse to the wagon. There are doubletrees and singletrees." The metal we had found was once attached to wood about the size of a baseball bat. I soon found a picture of one and recognized it immediately, as most people would. With the discovery of so many artifacts, I was beginning to learn a whole new vocabulary, the vocabulary of the 1800s.

3. The Hame Adjuster: There is a place in our museum for artifacts which I cannot identify. The place is labeled, 'Can you identify these?' Hopefully, someone will come through the museum and help me put a label on them. Grandson John found an object of cast iron about eight inches long with a ring at the end about the size of a silver dollar. The object had designed holes in it from one end to the other, and the ring was with the object, but not attached to it. This suggested that whatever the object was attached to had completely disentegrated in the ground. However, we did not have a clue as to what this object was a part of.

My good friend and neighbor, Bo Self, stopped by and when he saw this object, he said, "I can tell you exactly what this is. It's a hame adjuster. It's a part of the harness collar or yoke that fits over the horse's head and around his neck when the horse is about to pull something heavy. When pulling a plow, the hame adjuster helps determine the depth of the plow.

4. Wagonwheel hub rings: Evidently, wagonwheel rings, which gave support to the wooden hubs, would come off when the wooden hub would get too dry and shrink. We have found eight of these rings. My long time friend Bill Blythe (Robinson), told me that his family used to pull their wagons

into the creek, so that the axles and hubs would swell with a good soaking, and therefore prevent the rings from coming off.

5. <u>Cow and Oxen Bells:</u> We found a very large stock bell with the clapper still in it. Bill had also shared with me that in Texas in the 1850s, there were more oxen used for work that horses or mules.They were very strong animals. The large bell, he said, was probably an oxen bell. Also, since there were no fences, this was the best way to keep up with their animals.

6. <u>1913 Model T Ford magneto:</u> Vince dug deep, down by the creek in a location where we knew there was once habitation. The signal was unmistakable, it was iron. When we brought it up, I knew it was from a more recent time. It was a round disc about a foot in diameter, and had sixteen copper electrodes around the inside of the disc. We didn't have a clue as to what it was. I thought maybe it had something to do with the braking system on a train, since I knew trains had once been in the area. "There is a Railroad Museum in Galveston," I thought. "I will send them a photo, and maybe they can identify the artifact."The day after I contacted the Railroad Museum, I received an E-mail from Morris S. Gould, Executive Director of the Galveston Railroad Museum. Paraphrasing the e-mail, he said that the artifact had nothing to do with trains, but instead was a magneto(part of the hand-cranked ignition system) off of a Model T Ford.

Personal Items

The plantation comes to life most tenderly when we come face to face with a personal artifact which has been buried for many, many years. The reality of special moments which took place here burns deep into your imagination. Already mentioned is the gold ring, the 1858 silver half-dollar, and the 1899 five-cent piece.

1. <u>Little girl's turquoise lockett:</u> The metal detector beeped a faint signal, but strong enough to generate curiosity. The deeper I dug, the stronger the signal. I sifted through the dirt and found nothing. But then, at ten inches down, I saw what appeared to be a broken piece of blue glass. I picked it up, brushed it off some more, and realized it wasn't broken at all. It was heart shaped. The blue stone was inlaid in a silver

plated pendant, with part of the chain still on it. The treasure obviously belonged to some little girl who maybe received it for Christmas, a birthday gift, or some other special occasion. Her gift will be well taken care of, now that it lives again.

2. <u>White sapphire gold wedding ring:</u> Grandson Shannon, and his wife Meaghan enjoy coming up to hunt and dig for artifacts. Suddenly, we heard an unusual beep, so we put the shovel to work. 'Look, Grandpa,' Meaghan said, 'It's a ring!' It was slightly damaged, but the single stone was intact. We took it to a jeweler in Huntsville and had it completely restored. Two jewelers called the stone a white sapphire. It had the sparkle and beauty of a diamond, and the warm glow of 14kt. Gold.

3. <u>Cast iron lion 'still' penny bank:</u> Meaghan and I also found ½ of a small lion about four inches tall and five inches long. We went to the computer to search for information on this interesting little artifact. Research on the internet yielded a surprising answer. It turned out to be a penny bank, made between 1910 and 1920. The other half, no doubt, is still out there, somewhere.

4. <u>Indian head pennies:</u> Not long after finding the penny bank, we found pennies in the same area, dated 1905 and 1906.

My buddy, Jim Atherton, who owns a coin shop in old town Spring, north of Houston, had told me, 'The coins are coming!' He was right, and he was there to help me find them.

5. <u>The cast iron toy horse:</u> Many of the toys children played with in the late 1800s and early 1900s were made of cast iron. My daughter, Leah, reached down into the dirt and shouted, "Look Dad, it's a horse" Like the lion, it had split down the middle, and only half of the horse was there. Once again, we did not understand its purpose, or what it was part of. We did guess that it might be some kind of a toy. It had a place for a harness on it, so we figured it had a wagon attached to it. Again we searched the internet. I typed in, "antique cast iron toy horse" and the computer responded, "Wilkens Cast Iron Toys, made circa 1910, and there was a picture identical to the horse. It was pulling a fire wagon. A few days later I visited my neighbor, Bo Self, at his Diamond Bar Ranch. When I sat on the couch and looked up at the mantle on his fireplace, the

identical toy was there, completely painted and looking brand new. Bo had no idea that it had been made around 1910.

6. The cowboy's spur: The spur we found appears to be homemade, probably in the Robinson's blacksmith shop. In those days, spurs were a very useful personal item for the wrangler. It wasn't fancy, just made to really get that horse moving. It fit my boot perfectly. I bet the other spur is still out there waiting for someone to help it live again.

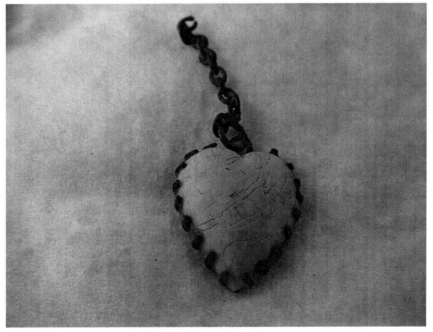

The blue pendant

White Sapphire
14kt gold wedding band

Cast iron penny 'still' bank

Homemade spur

Glassware

1. <u>Two coke bottles</u>-date 1915-Huntsville, Texas
2. <u>Two square "Soda Water" bottles</u>, Coca Cola Co.-date 1923-Huntsville, Texas.

We discovered that Coca Cola had opened several bottling plants in Texas in 1902, one being in Huntsville.

3. <u>Two medicine bottles</u>-"The name St. Joseph's assures pvrity" written on the side-Late 1800s.
4. <u>Three Levi Garrett snuff bottles.</u> Pat. Date, 1782.

The Push Broom

In August of 2010, I visited with Laura Henderson Robinson, a descendent who still lives in Point Blank. She had acquired some of the photos and paraphenalia from Libby who passed away in 2007. She allowed me to use some of the photos and clippings in my book project. Before I left, she went to her closet and brought to me an amazing artifact. It was a homemade push broom, which according to the Robinsons, was made by the slaves in the 1860s to sweep out the 'dog run' of our house. The handle was hand carved and the sweep was made of corn husks. It had belonged to Libby. Laura said, "I want to donate this to your museum. After all, your home is where it belongs." I could not thank her enough.

Chapter 6

State Archeological Site

With the museum intact, and the artifacts pouring in, I felt the need to let someone know who was a professional in the field of archeology, and even invite them to see what we had discovered. It was early January, 2010, when I called the anthropology department at Sam Houston State University in Huntsville, thinking that maybe they would like to come out and do a more scientific dig. They didn't seem to be that interested. The next day, however, I received a call from a lady at the Sam Houston Museum, which is close to the university. The anthropology department at Sam had notified her concerning my call. She introduced herself as Sandy Rogers, an 'archeological steward' for the State of Texas. The name sounded familiar, but I couldn't place her. She asked me not to do any more digging until she could come out to the plantation. This raised red flags in my mind. "What have I done,' I thought. 'I have alerted the authorities to my artifacts. They may come and take them away, and prevent me from digging on my own land anymore." My imagination began to run away with me. I went to my trusty computer and searched to find out just what a 'steward' was, and what were the laws in the state of Texas concerning artifacts found on private property. I was greatly relieved when I found out that an archeological steward simply assists and gives advice to the landowner in regards to artifacts, and the laws in Texas are very strong in favor of the landowner. Any artifact found on one's property is the sole posession of the landowner. With that in mind, I looked forward to her eventual visit.

A few weeks later, I received a call from Sandy. She would come for a visit and bring with her Don Keyes, the Director of Region 5 of the Texas Archeological Society. Point Blank was located in Region 5. Now I needed to polish up my little museum so it would make a good impression. Also, I didn't want them to think I was some redneck treasure hunter, but wanted them instead to think I was doing a responsible and semi-professional job. So I quickly joined the Texas Archeological Society, and made myself a certificate to hang in the museum. Also, I wanted to be able to say that I had a very accurate way of identifying the location of a found artifact. So I went to Walmart and bought a Global Positioning Satellite locater system, or GPS. I went back to the location of every item that we had found, and recorded the GPS longitude and latitude numbers, and since that time, I have recorded the location of every additional artifact found.

Left to Right: Bill West, Sandy Rogers, Don Keyes, Barbara West

I was ready for their visit, and as soon as I saw Sandy, we figured out that we had both worked for the Windham School System in Huntsville, many years earlier. I enjoyed taking her and Don through the museum and telling them all about the plantation, the artifacts, and the revealing research that I had done. They seemed impressed. Sandy said, "You know, Bill, what you need to do is order a Sears Roebuck catalogue from the late

1800s. Some of the items you are finding can be found in the catalogue."
I did as she suggested. I found an 1897 Sears catalogue on the internet for
$12.50. It has helped identify several unknown artifacts.

A few weeks later, on February 22nd, Sandy notified me that, through
their efforts, our property had been designated as a State Archeological
Site. We were given a trinomial identification number (41SJ223), meaning
that 41 represents the state of Texas, SJ is San Jacinto County, and we are
the 223rd archeological site in this county. I had no idea there were so many
archeological places in our county. Also, Sandy suggested that we might
like to designate an artifact rich area of our land as a State **Archeological**
Landmark or (SAL). It would mean that the State of Texas would have the
authority to do a professional dig on the said land, and would protect the
land for the owner of the property. We would still own the land, but the
state would have access to it. We said we would think about it. I wasn't sure
of all the legal ramifications. I just needed a little more time.

Sandy also said the state would provide a landmark plaque, similar to
the historical marker, to Barb and I for the land designation.

Homemade cornhusk broom
1860s

Chapter 7

The First Presentations

Both Sandy and I had retired years earlier from the Windham School System. She had gone to work as an archeological steward, and I went back to work teaching History, Physical Education, and coaching baseball for the Huntsville ISD. While the drama of the historical plantation unfolded, I was still teaching sixth graders at Huntsville Intermediate School. Excitedly, I began to take the more interesting relics to school to share with faculty, staff, and the children. My good friend and science teacher, Larry Fusaro, seemed very interested in the artifacts. He was also a Boy Scout troop leader. The 100th anniversary of the Boy Scouts of America was coming up. Larry asked if I would bring a display of artifacts to the Boy Scouts lodge on that Saturday. The lodge was a beautiful log cabin style structure, built in 1936. The anniversary was a huge celebration with many different activities going on. My son, Vince, joined me, and we spent the day showing and telling the scouts, their parents, and citizens of the city all about the plantation, the Robinsons, and the artifacts.

At the school, we were getting ready for Enrichment Day. This is a day set aside for the children to experience educational activities not normally seen at school. Guest presenters are invited to come to the school and present their special field of expertise, such as square dancing, outdoor cooking, and dog training. Director of Enrichment activities, Brian Gedelian, asked if I would be interested in providing a display of artifacts, and making a presentation to the children. I felt honored, and gave him a quick 'yes!'

I knew that to keep 5th & 6th graders captivated for 45 minute sessions was not going to be easy. So I asked myself, "What can I do to make this interesting to the kids, and keep them focused until the end?" I decided to invite an actual Robinson descendent, Bill Blythe, to come and share his stories of plantation memories. When Enrichment Day came, I was prepared with a plan. We had a nice display, complete with the most interesting artifacts, photos, and illustrations. After the children were seated on the floor in front of us, I played a little guitar, and sang a few lines of Dixie. It was my way of introducing the idea of a plantation to them. I had one of the artifacts covered with a veil. This was the beautiful 1858 silver coin display in the glass case. I told the children that the boy or girl who was the very best listener at the end of the session would be selected to unveil the 'secret' artifact. What they didn't know was that this 'secret' artifact was sitting on top of a bowl of chocolate candy kisses. After a brief explanation concerning the discoveries, I turned the program over to Bill. He kept them on the edge of their seats with stories about the plantation. For example, he remembered that on Christmas eve, to get the children to bed early, including himself, a Robinson adult would climb to the top of the chimney and shake and rattle Christmas bells so the children inside the living room would hear them. To the children, this meant that Santa had arrived on top of the roof, and it was time for them to get into bed." Enrichment Day was a great success!

Bill Blythe & Bill West
School Presentation
March, 2010

Display at Huntsville Intermediate School 2010

I found that I really enjoyed giving these presentations. I enjoyed telling about the artifacts and about the history of the plantation. The response I had received from both adults and children was better than I had anticipated. The notion came to me that if I would like to share our discoveries with more groups and individuals, that maybe I should create a website. With the help of the internet, I was able to create my own inexpensive website. It became: thewestriverplantation.homestead.com. I think the old house would approve, and it would be just another way to breathe life back into the plantation, whose memory had been fading fast, until the discovery of the artifacts. An article written in 1975 in the San Jacinto Times newspaper, by local writer and historian, Mrs. R. H. Blalock, and entitled, 'A History of Point Blank, emphasized the fact that even then, the little town's history was fading away. It read:

The heritage of Point Blank is fast disappearing, but it should be remembered and kept in the minds of its descendents, for the heroic struggle of the pioneers, who came here to establish a home, faced floods, death, loneliness, and hard work.

Chapter 8

The Field Trips

Our Principal at Huntsville Intermediate School, Angee Andrus, had seen the artifacts at the presentation, and heard some of the history of the plantation. This prompted a discussion between the two of us that a field trip to the plantation for the fifth graders might be a fun and educational experience. Late in each spring, educational field trips are pretty much the norm. There are two grades at the school, fifth and sixth. Most of the sixth graders had seen the artifacts at the presentation, but the fifth graders had not. A field trip for 400 fifth graders was then planned. Point Blank, being only twenty miles from Huntsville was a good choice for the teachers. It meant they didn't have to ride very far on the school buses with so many excited fifth graders.

There were three different trips planned for April, and a variety of activities planned for the kids. There would be fishing, pond study, geo-caching, kickball, tree hugging, history, hayrides, and an archeological dig. The weather was great, the crimson clover spread across the plantation, and the fish were biting. My assignment was to take them on a historical tour through the home, and the museum, and then take them on a hayride where they could do some actual digging.

When each group would come to me, I would sit them down in front of the historical marker and tell them this story: "This house, and this land, boys and girls has a lot of history behind it, dating all the way back to General Sam Houston's time, 150 years ago. It belonged to one family, the Robinsons, for 120 years. They grew lots of cotton here, loaded it on steamboats, and shipped it down the Trinity River to Galveston, and across the ocean to Europe. You see, boys and girls, right through those trees over there across the highway is the river." I glanced over my shoulder a time or two, and the old house seemed to have a great big smile. I continued, "When you look at the house, what you see is nothing like the way it looked in 1857 when it was built. It is actually a log house, made of solid cypress logs. They were hewed out with axes, and interlocked together." One curious little boy interrupted, "Did they have slaves in those days?, Coach West." My answer, "Yes, they did, for about the first eight years. It was a sad part of American history, but it was true." I continued, "There was also a veranda, or balcony, across the front and the back. In 1915 however, the house was remodeled. The logs were covered with the present day siding that you see, and the balconies were taken down. The logs are still there, just covered up. You can, however, look under the house and see those huge timbers. They are one foot square, interlocked, and stretch all the way across the house. You can still see the axe marks in them. When you tour the house in a few minutes, notice the corners of the rooms. They come together at a 45 degree or slant angle, not the regular 90 degree corners you see in most houses. Those are the huge verticle timbers which give support to the walls of the house." When we toured the house, I pointed out the hand carved railing on the stairway and some of the archetecture. When we entered the large kitchen, I explained that in the 1800s, this was not the kitchen. It was the dining room. The kitchen, where they prepared the food, was outside the house. In those days, with no air conditioning, it was too hot to have the stove in the house. The kids seemed interested, but, without exception, they were more interested in the chocolate chip cookies on the table that Mrs.West had prepared for them.

Field Trip Fishing
2010

Field Trip- Bill West
Sharing Plantation History

Field Trip Hayride

The next stop was the museum. We gathered in front of the two-story barn, and there I began my speech: "Before we go up to the museum, boys and girls, I want you to remember this---until just a few months ago, many of the artifacts you will see lay buried for up to 150 years. It is as though they are saying to us, 'Oh thank you, thank you, thank you for setting us free from the deep, dark, dungeon of the underworld. Thank you for letting us see the light of day once again, and the smiling faces of these wonderful children.' Who could deny the plantation was beginning to live again? I continued with my speech, "When these artifacts fell into the ground, children, the world you see around you was completely different. There were no electric lights, cell phones, no automobiles, no computers, no i-pods, no air planes, no telephones, no televisions, and no air conditioning. Think their lives were boring? Not at all! They rode horses, went swimming, went hunting and fishing, climbed trees, had races, went dancing, played baseball, had family reunions, and families prayed together, and stayed together. On the other hand, the first Robinsons to live here would be absolutely stunned if they could walk into the house today and see all of the modern conviences.

Now we are going up into the museum. The best way to get the most out of it is to take the time to read about the artifact and/or look at the photos which illustrate its purpose." The children seemed fascinated as they walked through, viewing the discoveries. Some of them shared with me the fact that they had found artifacts on their own land. As they exited the museum, I instructed them to 'go jump on the hay wagon and we would go for a ride. I didn't have to tell them twice. With tractor and wagon, I drove them to an area where I had found artifacts before. "Ok, boys and girls, we're going to do a little digging," I said. They were ecstatic. I showed them how to use the metal detector, and how we would record our discoveries if we found anything. Unfortunately, we didn't find anything of museum quality, but they had fun digging, and they learned a little archeological procedure.

All three field trips were an absolute success, and we were all relieved there were no injuries, or accidents. When the children left, I looked back at the old house, and said, "Well, what do you think?" I believe the response came in a great big smile of approval. In the week following the field trips I received 400 thank you notes to Mrs. West and myself. To us, the visit by the boys and girls had been a wonderful experience. What better way to bring the plantation back to life than to see and hear so many children laughing, playing, and having fun. The plantation would live again, but this time in complete harmony of all races of people, and void of slavery. The discovery of the artifacts had made this possible. Below are just a few of the many 'Thank you' notes that we received from the fifth graders:

Dear Coach West and Mrs. West, I thank you for leting us come to your house. I loved fishing I had allmost caugth Grandaddy blue. I had hem over the water then he let go. I loved learning about your land and house. I also loved the story about Sam Hustion's gost during the wenter. I also loved the hayride. I loved looking at your treasure.

P. S. I loved your dog and I hope you find more teasure. I also thank Mrs. West for the cookies.

Sincerly,
Michaela

Dear Coach West,
Thank you for letting us come to your house for our field trip. I really enjoyed all the activities we did, but my favorite one was when we went through your museum and saw all the interesting things you and your wife found in your yard.

Sincerely,
Kirstyn

Dear Coach West and Mrs. West,
thank you for allowing us to have this field trip on your property. I learned a lot more about nature. Even though I used to go camping a lot. This way the best field trip I've went on this whole year. This was my first experiance of fishing. At least I think it is. The cookies were delicous. The stuff that you dug up. it was very interesting. Thank you!!!

Sincerely, HIS
Auriauna

Dear Coachwest and Mrs. West,
Thank you for leting us go in your house and leting us go on your tractor too. And the fishing too. Pluse the dog was so cute. And diging up all that stuff and looking at all that artifacts. And the GPSes.

Thank you,
your friend, Joe

Thack yoll for let us for coming. I love all the activedes and I Thack Coach west and Mrs. West. I and the team won The kickball. I cot 22 fish and I love the musim. I Thanck Mrs west for the cookes thay were good.

Sencerely,
Katie

Thank you Coach West for inviting us to river plantation. I have always wanted to see a real plantation. We liked the cookies too. Thanks for inviting us.

Thanks,
Caitlyn

Coach West,
Thank you so much for allowing my peers to come to River Plantation! I enjoyed every bit of the field trip. I thought the museum was very neat! I espesally loved fishing. I caught 3 fish. I know that all my friends had a great time!!

Thank you,
Blake

Coach West and Mrs. West,
I had a great time at your house discovering things and having fun playing games. All six activities were awesome and the only way to have them all was at your house.

Thank you,
Zac

Chapter 9

Summer of 2010

San Jacinto County Historical Commission

It was close to midnight on that hot August evening in 1978 when we rolled onto the plantation property in those two u-haul vans. We had permission from the Robinsons to store our furniture and things in the barn until the deal for the plantation was final.

Suddenly, there were flashing lights, and I asked myself, "What is this, a police car pulling up right behind us?" A young officer stepped out of his patrol car and introduced himself. "Hello, my name is Officer Magee. Looks like you folks are moving in," he said. I responded politely, "Well, not yet. We're just going to store our things here until the deal is consummated." He was there at the request of the Robinsons to keep an eye on the place and watch over it. He asked whether we needed any assistance. I said 'no thanks, and he left. That was the first time that I had met Gregg Magee, and he was the first person we met after coming home. We would become life-long friends. Eventually, he would become a lawyer, and then Justice of the Peace in Point Blank.

One day in early June, I said to my wife, Barbara, "You know, we ought to invite Greg and his wife, Betty, over to see the museum. They've been in Point Blank a long time, and I bet they would like to see it." She responded, "That's a good idea. I think Betty has something to do with the Historical Comission in Coldspring." So I gave them a call, and they came over the same afternoon. They were impressed. Betty explained that she was chairman of the San Jacinto County Historical Commission, and she thought they would be very much interested in what we had found.

A few days later, Betty came again, and brought with her another member of the SJCHC, Dale Evritt. Dale thought the finds were significant, and suggested that the local newspaper, <u>The San Jacinto News-Times</u> might be interested in writing an article so other people in the county would be aware of the discoveries. We were then invited to participate in the historic celebration of the 140th Anniversary of San Jacinto County. It would be held in August at the VFW hall in Camilla, Texas, not far from Point Blank.

San Jacinto County Historical Commission Meeting
Left to right - Judy Schreiner, Rose Marie Leisner, Bill West, Betty Magee, Vince West, Billie Trapp

Application for the State Archeological Landmark

By mid July, Barb & I had given a lot of thought to the idea of designating a portion of land, as Sandy had suggested, as a State Archeological Landmark. It would be nice to have a professional dig executed at the plantation. They have a degree of expertise which could provide a more detailed explanation of the way things used to be. Also,

I needed help and guidance concerning my own methods. Besides, this would be just another way to pump life back into the old plantation.

I e-mailed Sandy and informed her of our intentions. In a few days she and Don Keyes returned, and we all decided on a one-acre plot of land as a State Archeological Landmark. The application would have to be approved by the state, and would probably take a couple of months for completion.

The Old Jail Museum in Coldspring

"Hey Dad," Vince said, "did you know there used to be a picture of our house hanging in the courthouse in Coldspring?" "No son, I didn't," I responded. Evidently, when the kids were in high school in the early 80s, they saw this picture hanging in a small museum housed in the courthouse, but in 1983 the museum was moved to the old jail facility in Coldspring. The building was no longer used as a jail. I thought it would be nice if we could find the old photo. It was taken before the verandas were removed, according to our children. Sometimes Betty Magee goes to do volunteer work at the old Museum, so I ask her if I could come down and go through some of the old photos which were not on display. She said yes. I met her there on a Saturday morning, and we spent a couple of hours looking for that picture, but to no avail. However, in one old box Betty found a set of photos showing the ceremony in 1975 of the Robinson house becoming a State **Historical** Landmark. While searching, I realized that the Old Jail Museum is rich in historical records, articles, maps and photos which date back to the mid 1800s. There has to be valuable information there concerning the history of the old plantation. I then made plans for more visits to this interesting and historic building.

Topographical Accuracy

In late July, I stopped by the Sam Houston Museum in Huntsville to visit with Sandy. "I have a question for you, Sandy. Is there a type of map which has latitude and longitudinal lines at a very small scale, like within a few feet?", I asked. She responded, "You could order a topographical map from topo.com, but I'm not sure what the scale will be.You could also make one of your own, just for your property." I explained,"What I would like to be able to do is record the name of the found artifacts on a scale map, instead of using the datum point method I've been using." When I arrived home, I went to the internet and ordered a topographical map of Point Blank. It was a nice map, but the scale was too large for my purpose.

I needed one just for the plantation, the scale lines within a few feet of each other. I was faced with making one of my own. This has become an ongoing project. In the end, I want a visual chart that identifies all the items found and where they were found, accurate within a few feet. This is separate from the GPS system, which of course, has pinpoint accuracy.

Chapter 10

A Visit With Bess and Bill Blythe Robinson

In early August, Barb and I were priviledged to visit the Houston home of ninety-six year old Bess, Granddaughter of Tod Sr., Great granddaughter of Robert Tod Robinson, and wife of Colonel William Jackson Blythe, this Southern lady is a true belle of the South, gracious and Victorian in every aspect. She is a living witness to almost 100 years of growth and development in Point Blank, and San Jacinto County. Her son, Bill, who is a former state representative, also joined us.

Memories

"Barb, what were some of those questions we were going to ask Bess and Bill?,"I asked. Barb responded, "Well, instead of starting with questions, why don't we just let Bess share some of her childhood memories of Point Blank"" Bess began, "When Robert Tod died, my grandfather, Tod Sr., took over the estate and the management of the property. When he got married, he built the house that I was raised in. It was located across the highway and down toward the creek. You see, Robert Tod's wife and some of their children were still living in the house that you do. My grandfather's house was a large Victorian style, five bedroom, single story structure with a rap around porch. There were lots of flowers, flowers everywhere. They called it the 'big house.' Headquarters for the plantation, so to speak, shifted from the Robert Tod house to my grandfather's new house.

I was born in Lowndesboro, near Montgomery, Alabama, and was brought to Point Blank when I was one year old. My father's family, the

Tysons, owned a huge plantation in Alabama, with a beautiful Greek Revival house. It was adorned with sixteen circular columns. I was born in that house." I shared with her the fact that the West family also came from Alabama in the 1800s. My grandfather was born in Phoenix City, Alabama. Barb asked Bess, "What about your mother and father?" Bess said, "My mother was Fannie Rose Robinson, and she met my father, Thomas Tyson when she was in Alabama visiting the Robinson family. They became engaged, and when my mother finished college, they were married in Point Blank. They had a very big wedding.'Where in Point Blank were they married?," I asked. Bess continued,"In the church. We had a church there, and a drugstore, and a 'Woodsmen of the World' two story building, and my grandfather's store, and a saloon. They were all lined up there together, and it was quite a thriving little community." Barb asked, "What about brothers and sisters, did you have any?" Bess responded, "I had a brother, Tom Jr., who is now passed. He was 14 years younger than I. I was like a mother to him. I just adored him."Barb continued, "What about your education? Where did you go to school?" Bess replied, "In Point Blank. We had a school there. It was located in the church. We went to school through the seventh grade in Point Blank. After that, I went to high school in Huntsville at the Sam Houston State Normal school, until my last year. I went to the high school in Oakhurst in my senior year, where I became **Valdictorian.**

Bess Tyson Blythe Robinson

"Did they still raise a lot of cotton in Point Blank when you were a child, and could you see the river from the house, Bess?," I asked. Bess responded,"Yes, they did raise a lot of cotton, but no, you could not see the river from the house. Do you know where the big bridge is that crosses the lake now?" All the property from your house to the bridge was owned by my grandfather. He gave my mother all the land that is now called Point Lookout Estates for a wedding present. Cotton was grown from your house all the way to the big bridge, but you couldn't see the river from the land until you got close to the water." Barb then asked Bess, "I guess the original 3500 acres was gradually split up among family members, was it?" Bess replied, "Yes, Major Robinson had originally bought the land from O. M. Wheeler, who owned a sugar cane planation. The land was reduced somewhat during my grandfather's time, although the plantation prospered very well. He was a generous man. In fact, the Robinsons were a very generous family. One of his donations went to the black community for the cemetery across the highway from you, which bears his name, The Tod Robinson Cemetery."

Barb then turned to Bill and asked, " Before Libby passed away, she told us that part of the Robinson land was bought from Governor Wood. How does that fit in?" Bill responded, "Governor Wood also lived in this area, and I think the Robinsons probably bought land from both Wood and Wheeler."

The Tyson Plantation
birthplace of Bess Robinson
Lowndesboro, Alabama

Before 1857?

Barb then asked, "We've been curious about the date on the historical marker, which says the house was built in 1857. Libby had told us that she thought the house was built several years earlier. What do you think, Bess?" Bess responded, "Well, Robert Tod was born in 1836 to Major William Robinson. William had come out to Texas prior to the 1830s, and had a land grant from Mexico. Then, he started buying land. He returned to Alabama and then brought three of his sons back to Texas to settle here." Bill interjected, "Let's back up for just a moment. There was an uncle to the Robert Tod who built your house. The uncle was from North Carolina, and his name was also Tod Robinson, one of several Robinsons from this family whose middle name was Tod. His brother was William. The uncle came out first and settled down in Brazoria County. After 1836, he served in the Republic of Texas Congress. William came out shortly after Tod, and bought some land over by Oakhurst close to Raven Hill, next to where Sam Houston lived. William didn't stay there long before he bought land at Point Blank. This was during the Republic, about 1840. The possibility of your home being built prior to 1857 is probable. You can go back to the deed records, and they will tell the story. Of course we're talking about deed records in three different counties, because San Jacinto County was created from a part of Liberty, Polk, and Walker counties." Barb continued to question Bess, "I was thinking it had to be before 1857 because Robert Tod was married in what ,1854? They had their first child in 1856, didn't they? Surely, they had the house built by then. I pulled some information off the internet, and didn't Robert Tod marry a lady by the name of Mary Louise McGowen?" Bess responded,"Yes, he did. She was from Camilla, close to Coldspring. The McGowen family also owned a plantation along the Trinity."

I turned to Bill at this point, and asked, "One of the questions we have is about Robert Tod. We visited the Robinson Cemetery in Point Blank last Sunday, and were able to account for the five generations of Robinsons, except Robert Tod himself. Why is he not buried there, and where was he laid to rest?" Bill answered quickly, "Camilla! You see, Mary died young, at the age of 32, and so she was buried in her family's cemetery at Camilla. They had six children, so naturally the children were going to have their father buried alongside their mother when Robert Tod passed away. Besides, he probably requested it."

"Bess, do you recall seeing any steamboats on the Trinity when you were growing up," I asked. Bess answered, "You see, we didn't really live that close to the river. So I don't remember seeing any. But I do remember something else. The Trinity often overflowed its banks, and the water would then come up close to the house. One time when that happened, an alligator swam close to the house, and our mechanic, Sam, lassoed the alligator. But the alligator was too strong and Sam had to let go. I remember that very well."

The Truth-Point Blank

There have been many rumors concerning how the little town of Point Blank got its name. Bill mentioned that some folks falsely believed that the outlaw, John Wesley Hardin, hid out down at 'Devils Half-acre', close to Point Blank and shot someone 'point blank.' Another story suggested that the name had something to do with race, which, of course, could not be further from the truth. "Bill, how much truth is there to the story that the French governess, Florence Dissosway, was responsible for the town's name?,"I asked. Bill answered, "It's pretty much a historical fact. Here's the reason. When she approached the Robinson land, which stretched from where the big bridge is today all the way to beyond Governor's Point subdivision, she could see lots of cotton and referred to it as the pont blanc, French for white point." Bess then added, "Let me tell you the story. I have heard all my life that Grandfather had a French governess. So when I married my husband, I told him the story, and he asked, 'Where in the world would you get a French governess in the wilds of Texas?' I told him that I didn't know. So being quite curious, my husband, Jack, went over to Liberty County where he had heard there was a French settlement, to see if he could locate any Dissosways. There were none. He also searched other French settlements close by, but to no avail. It wasn't long after that, we were in Alabama visiting family. My husband, Jack, or as you know him, Colonel Blythe, was introduced by the Robinsons there to the next door neighbor. His name was Dissosway, the same family from which Florence came so many years ago. Major William Robinson had asked Florence's father to grant permission for her to go to Texas to educate the Robinson grandchildren." Bill added, "Again, you can go back to the deed records and the name is spelled, 'Pont Blanc.' Bess continued, "It was Tod Sr., Robert Tod's son, who applied for the first post office in Point Blank. This was in 1884. When he applied, he spelled the name Pointe Blanc. In Washington however, assuming that Texans didn't know how to spell, they scratched through the French spelling and made it Point Blank. We have a copy of that record in Huntsville."

The Well, Wagon Road, Gristmill, and the Dairy

"Where was the draw well located in relation to the plantation house, Bess?" I asked. As you face the house, it was to the left, right where the cherokee roses grew." I added, "That's what Libby had said in our conversation with her years ago.You know Bess, those roses were still growing there until we cleared the fence line a few months ago. So I have a pretty good idea where it is located. Some archeologists say that's a good place to look for artifacts. I need to check that out."

Bill added,"Close to that old well area, you will see a dip in the land. That was the old wagon road. It came right up close to the house. It went right through the middle of your land and crossed the creek down in the corner close to the present day bridge on Highway 156." I thought to myself, "That fits, because I have found several horse and wagon artifacts along that old road, like wagon wheel rings, axle sleeves, and buggy seat springs." Bill continued, "Right there where you cross the creek, when I was growing up, you could still see the old pylons from Robert Tod's gristmill. Tod Sr. also had a gristmill, but it was up behind Glover's place on Mill Creek. In fact, years ago, they found the stone to Tod's gristmill. Bess added, "Besides the gristmill, there was also a sawmill there close to the gristmill. Tod Sr. had bought it from one Thomas Snow." In reflection, I wondered, "That must be how Snow Hill Road got it's name. It's along the ridge above us, possibly named after Thomas Snow." I always figured, mistakenly, that it had to do with snowy weather.

Bill added more to the conversation, "There is something else you might like to know in relation to your property. Right where Lee Walker's house is located, to the right and front of the plantation house, there was a black family who lived there in the 1860s. This was Robinson land. Do you remember their names, Mom?" Bess answered, "Aunt Mariah, and Uncle Ned Richardson. Aunt Mariah was in charge of the dairy, which was located close to the 'big house.' The people who did the milking would come to Aunt Mariah and she would give them what they needed to milk the cows. They could not enter the dairy without her permission. She was the boss. Even the cook could not go into the dairy without asking Aunt Mariah first."Barb commented, "The black family were no longer slaves, but more like employees, weren't they?" Bill answered, "No, they were more like family to the Robinsons." Bess added, "There was a special bond between the Robinsons and the black community."

The Slavery Issue

"You know, Bill,' I asked, 'The slave era at the plantation only lasted about eight years, from 1857 to 1865, unless of course the house was built before 1857. What did the negro people do after the war, stay there and work for the right to stay on the land, or just what did they do?" Bill answered, "Well, the Robinsons had a reputation for protecting the black people. In fact, my mother's black friend, who is now in the cemetery, wrote how the Robinsons protected and took care of her family. The Robinsons would not let anybody abuse them. Probably what happened was that our family either gave them or sold them patches of land to live on. Also, Tod Robinson permitted a black man, whom he liked very much, to have a store across the street (on Robinson land), to compete against his own store. It was quite OK with Tod. They were friends." Bess intervened to support what Bill was saying. She opened the book entitled, *San Jacinto County Cemetery Records, The Tod Robinson Cemetery.* It read:

"The Tod Robinson Cemetery was started as a burial place for the persons of color that occupied the Robinson Quarters. Many people lived in the Quarters due to the protective net the Quarters offered them by the Robinsons. It was understood that Mr. Robinson protected all residents and made sure they were treated well, women were given respect, and all were paid fairly.

Due to this measure of protection, people were moving here from other communities of the county, to take advantage of the Quarters, and its protection measures instituted. This protection was given due to the Jim Crow Laws (note: having to do with the practice or unwritten policy to segregate races in public places such as restaurants, buses, schools, etc.) that repented the rights that were given after the Emancipation Proclamation. **The famed Eddie Robinson (1919-2007), Coach of Grambling University, Louisiana, is a descendent of the Quarters.**

From another local source, we were told that Mr. Robinson, at the end of slavery, offered a choice to the men and women who worked for him. Each adult could either take the deed to 40 acres of rich farm land each, or he would give the men $750.00, and a horse, saddle and gun, and they could go where they pleased. For the women, he offered the same, except instead of horse and saddle, they could have a wagon and a span of mules. This source said that some took one offer while others took the other offer. Some of those who took the 40 acres found themselves quite well off when the lake was built. Remember, this is oral history, which sometimes gets slightly changed after being told many times. Regardless, this cemetery has a rich and colorful history."

Barb continued, "We received an E-mail recently from long time teacher and historian, Billie Trapp, in Coldspring, that according to the 1860 census, Robert Tod owned fifty slaves, while his brother, Henry, owned forty-one." Bill spoke up and said, "I've seen those numbers, and, in my opinion, they are small. I think they owned many more, or another possibility is that there were free men and women available to be hired. I know Major Robinson in Alabama owned close to six hundred, and Tyson had four to five hundred. So knowing how many workers they had in Alabama per number of acres, Robert Tod and Henry would need a lot more help than the census indicated in order to run a cotton plantation." Bess had heard enough of this talk of slavery. She interrupted, and stated emphatically, "The Robinsons did not believe in slavery per se. They did not call them, or refer to them as slaves. In fact, they brought some of these folks with them when they came from Alabama to Texas, like Aunt Mariah, and Uncle Ned. The Robinsons helped their black friends and family become more independent. In more recent years, there was a black family living on what is now your land. Their home was by those crepe myrtles next to the creek. I remember their names were Granny and Gabe Jones. It was their great- grandaughter who became the first black female student at Rice University in Houston.

Sam Houston, Governor Wood, and Robert Tod

"Bess, Libby had said years ago that General Houston, Governor Wood, and Robert Tod danced with the ladies in the 'dog run' of our house (which is now the foyer). Is this true? Did those three frontiersmen really hang out with each other a lot, and do you know this for sure?" Barb asked. Bess responded, "Yes! The three of them often visited and socialized together. In spite of their verifications, educational, and military backgrounds, they became close friends. Their homes were in reasonably close proximity to each other." Bill interjected, "You see, Sam Houston used to come to Point Blank from his home at Raven Hill, and stay at the plantation house, or stay with an Indian tribe at Stephens Creek, then catch a steamboat to Houston (Harrisburg)".

Oakhurst and Snowtown

Barb continued with her questions, "Bess, we've always heard that Oakhurst, which is only a community now with a just a Post Office, was once a thriving little town, with a hotel and a movie theater. Is that true?" Bess replied, "Yes, Oakhurst was really a sawmill town. They had two large sawmills there. There was also a little town nearby called Snowtown. I remember it well because they had the best hamburgers there. The man who made them had his own little hamburger stand, and he was a very big guy. But in Oakhurst they had a commissary, a doctor, a bakery, an ice house, and they had what we called a picture show. The reel of the film would break down and we would just have to sit there and wait. The lights were out and we would have to wait for them to come back on, but we didn't mind. We were young and it was fun to sit there in the dark." Bill intervened and said, "There used to be a guy who would come to Point Blank in a truck that had a traveling picture show. He would let all the children and adults know he was there, so when they all gathered around, he would drop a screen down at the back of the truck and show everyone a picture show. We would pay him five or ten cents each to watch the show."

I commented to Bill that I had never heard of Snowtown. Later, I found that Snowtown was a thriving little sawmill town in the late 1800s, very close to Oakhurst. Betty Magee, Chairman of the San Jacinto County Historical Comission, loaned me a historical booklet written in 1992. It was entitled *San Jacinto County, A Glimpse Into the Past.*It had an article in it that read:

History of Snowtown—1872: Snowtown---have you ever heard of it? It was a thriving little town until good roads were built and people began to go to the city to trade. Then, when the Oakhurst sawmill shut down and the people moved from the mill yards, the post office was brought to Snowtown, and people began calling the little town Oakhurst. Snowtown was in the eastern part of Walker County, until San Jacinto county was organized December 1ˢᵗ , 1870. San Jacinto County was founded from portions of Polk, Liberty, Montgomery, and Walker Counties. After the new county was founded, Snowtown was in the north eastern part of San Jacinto County.

Snowtown didn't have a post office. They didn't need one. The earlier settlers didn't write much, and they received very little mail. Their mail came to Dodge, and they picked it up once a month.

In the year of 1899, a post office was established at the little sawmill town of Oakhurst. Since Snowtown was only ¼ mile to Oakhurst, the settlers had their mail changed to Oakhurst. The mail was first carried by horse back from Dodge. A few years later the mail came to Point Blank, and was carried by horseback to Oakhurst. The Oakhurst Company needed their men to work at the mill, so they agreed to let the Snowtown men carry the mail. W. J. Clark carried the mail for a number of years. J. M. Dolive also carried the mail a long time.

Snowtown was named after Thomas H. Snow, one of the early settlers.

Snow ran a store and a saloon there. He went by ox wagon to Huntsville and bought his merchandise to sell. It took him three days to make the trip.

When liquor was voted out of Snowtown, Snow sold his store, and moved to Rough Edge, five miles south of Snowtown. He built a saloon and Tom Banks was his bartender. Later, he turned his saloon over to Banks, and moved a mile southeast of Point Blank, and farmed. He built a cotton gin and some years later after an accident in the gin , he bled to death.

Another one of Snowtown's settlers was A. A. Aden, a school teacher, who taught school at Swartout, in Polk County, in 1850. His salary depended on the number of students who were able to pay the ten cents charged each child per day. After his wife, Mary Sue Aden's death, he moved to Snowtown and built a home. He later married Rebecca Tanner of Walker County. Aden was elected San Jacinto County Surveyor in 1872, and Comissioner of Precinct 4 in 1882. Aden's old home in Snowtown has just recently been torn down.

Snowtown started growing in 1908, when the Oakhurst sawmill company bought the Palmetto sawmill and combined the two mills at Oakhurst. Some of the old settlers went to work at the sawmill. They bought a lot and built a house. Snowtown had a depot when a railroad was built from Oakhurst to Dodge. The train carried freight, mail, and passengers. It stopped at Snowtown to let the passengers off and on. It cost 10 cents to ride the train from Oakhurst to Snowtown, and 25 cents to ride from Snowtown to Dodge.

Barb continued, "We've heard that Oakhurst was bigger than Point Blank, that they even had a hotel there." Bill responded,"Yes, at one time. I remember as a kid, driving through Oakhurst at night, and the whole sky would be lit up from the burning of the sawdust." Bess added, "They also had a train to come through there, and you could take the train from Oakhurst to Dodge, Texas, and from there to Houston." Bill then commented, "Actually, they got the trains closer to Point Blank than that. Oakhurst is six miles from Point Blank, and they had 'tram tracks' leading from Oakhurst to Snow Town to Coldspring, which came fairly close to Point Blank. You can still see parts of the old tram track system up on Snow Hill. For example, if Tod Sr. had ordered some heavy equipment for his cotton gin, they could get fairly close with it to Point Blank, and deliver it by oxen from there.

Barb continued with the next question, "Were these two sawmills responsible for the clearing of the land? That is, did they leave wide areas of land deforested so that lots of cotton could be grown." Bill answered, "Actually, while there was a lot of timberland, there was also a lot of small farms which had cleared lots of land. Then, when hard times hit, many of the farmers moved to the cities, and the lumber companies came in and bought up the land. So a lot of the land that was once cleared is now forest land. My mother remembers standing on the front porch of the 'big house' and seeing the sky lit up over Conroe, which is fifty miles to the south. What she saw were the flames from the oil fields. She could see it because so much land was cleared. You take, for example, the national forest and the Gibbs family, a very prominent and wealthy family in Huntsville. The Gibbs had lots and lots of land. They sold their land to the federal government, which helped to establish the Sam Houston National Forest.

Those Robinson Boys:
Major William, Uncle Tod, Robert Tod, Henry, Cornelius, Gilbert,
& Young William

"Sons, I leave this land to you. I am confident that you and your families will prosper well. May God be with you." These could have been the parting words from Major William Robinson when he left Robert Tod, Henry, and Gilbert in Point Blank, Texas, to return to his wife, Eliza Jane, in Alabama. When William wrote his last will and testament, he left no doubt about his intentions for the three eldest sons. Following is a copy of a part of William's will provided to me by Bill. It reads:

State of Alabama
Lowdes County
May 13, 1878

In the Name of God, Amen. I, William Robinson, of the County and State aforesaid, being of sound mind and disposing memory, do make, sign, and publish this writing as my last will and testament as follows:

1st: That it is my wish and desire as soon after my death,

as it can convieniently be done, that all my just debts be paid from the moneys of my Estate.

2nd: I give and bequeath to my children (in Texas) Robert T. Robinson, Henry W. Robinson, and Gilbert Robinson my entire interests in all my lands in the State of Texas, to be equally divided between each, to share and share alike in said lands, to have and to hold to their separate use, and they or neither of them shall be required to account to my Estate for any profits, rents, or income from said land...

William Robinson

The boys were young and up to the task, and so they began to build the Robinson plantation. Robert Tod would soon marry Mary McGowen of Camilla, and would build the house from which I am writing this book. Robert Tod and his brother Henry, worked hard to make the plantation prosperous, while Gilbert returned to Alabama when the Civil War broke out.

Uncle Tod

In the meantime, Major William's brother, Tod Robinson (Uncle Tod) 1812-1870), was making a name for himself in other parts of Texas, and in California. In Galveston, he became one of the founding members of the Episcopal Church of 1839, the oldest church in Galveston. An article written in The Handbook of Texas Online, *"Tod Robinson"*, by Thomas Cutrer, gave a brief description of Unlce Tod's life:

Tod Robinson, lawer and legislator, was born on March 1, 1812, in Anson County, North Carolina, and soon moved with his parents to Alabama. He immigrated to Texas in February 1839, after several years residence in New Orleans, and settled on San Luis Pass opposite the lower end of Galveston Island. There, later that year, he and Matthew Hopkins established and edited the San Luis *Advocate*. In 1841 Robinson was elected to represent Brazoria County in the House of Representatives of the Sixth Congress of the Republic of Texas, where he served as Chairman of the Committee on finance. In 1842 he served in Captain John

P. Gills company of Colonel Clark L. Owens regiment in the campaign against Rafael Vasquez. Robinson was reelected to the Seventh Congress of 1842, and to the Ninth in 1844. He was a strong advocate of annexation. He moved to California in 1849 or 1850, presumably in the rush for gold, leaving his wife, the former Mary Judith Crittenden of Galveston, in Texas. In California he became a prominent Whig politician. He moved for a time to Virginia City, Nevada, but returned to California, where he died in San Mateo County, on October 27, 1870.

Letter From Sam Houston to Tod Robinson

To my astonishment, Bill and Bess provided me with a copy of a letter from General Houston to Tod Robinson in 1842, when Tod was Chairman of the Finance Committee for the Republic of Texas. This is only six years after the fall of the Alamo, and the battle at San Jacinto. Houston was requesting funds to help 'procure and maintain peace' with the Indians. The letter is from *The Writings of Sam Houston,* compiled and edited by Amelia Williams and B C Barker, Volume LV (pages 69-70), *Writings of Sam Houston, 1842.* The letter reads:

General Sam Houston

To Tod Robinson

Executive Department
City of Austin   January 5, 1842

To the Honorable Tod Robinson
Chairman of the Committee on Finance:

In reply to your note of this morning, I have to state most respectfully, that the amount heretofore usually appropriated for the service of this Department as Executive Contingent Fund, and for the use of the Executive Office, will probably be required for the present year.

It is a matter of much interest to me, and perhaps of equal moment to the Country that I should have the means of procuring and maintaining peace with the Indians on any borders. With this object in view, I should be much gratified to have an appropriation of some fifteen or twenty thousand dollars as an Indian fund: to be acccounted for as other moneys for the expenditure of which vouchers are required. If this is done, and power given to restrain whites from misconduct toward them, I will answer for the safety of our frontiers.

Sam Houston

A Family Tradition

At this point, my curiosity got the best of me and I asked Bess, "Is there some special reason, or tradition as to why so many of the Robinson boys have the middle name, "Tod?" Bess replied, "Yes, there is. There was a young lady in the late 1700s whose last name was Todd, and she married a Robinson. Not to lose her family name, she gave her son the middle name of Tod, and then it became a tradition in the Robinson family."

As we continued our conversation with Bill and Bess, they began to share more of their memories concerning those first Robinson brothers who met the challenge of taming the wilderness of early Texas.

Henry, and Cornelius Ware Robinson

Barb asked Bess, "Would you tell us a little about Henry? Bess responded, "Well, Henry lived in the house that had been Governor Wood's house. The Robinsons had bought the house and the land that Governor Wood owned." Bill added, "Henry had a son named Cornelius (Neal) Robinson. Neal became a district judge here in Houston, and when he died, 12,000 people came to his funeral. Twelve thousand---and that was in the 1920s." At that point in our conversation, Bill handed me a clipping about Cornelius from *A History of Texas and Texans, Volume 4,* written many years ago, by Francis White Johnson and Ernest William Winkler:

The Honorable Cornelius Ware Robinson

The present judge of the criminal district court of Harris County got his training in the law while engaged in farming in one of the south Texas counties. He has been a hard worker all his life, and it was a steadfast ambition which led him from the restricted field of agriculture to the higher sphere of law and life. Born November 22, 1863, at <u>Point Blank</u>, in Polk County, but now in San Jacinto County, Texas, Judge Robinson is a son of Henry Ware and Annie (Goodall) Robinson. He is a descendent of prominent Alabama and Tennessee families. His great-uncle was Judge

Todd Robinson (Uncle Tod), who rose to distinction as a member of the Texas bar, from this state moved out to California, where he was elevated to the bench and became chief justice of the supreme court of California. Henry Ware Robinson was born in Alabama, came to Texas about 1855, settling at Point Blank, and as a business man was a planter and stock raiser. During the war, he went to the front with a Texas regiment, and after the struggle was over, returned and took up the quiet vocations of country life. Annie Robinson was of a Tennessee family, whose members were long prominent in that state.

Judge Robinson was educated at the Agricultural and Mechanical College in Bryan, and in Baylor University while located at Independence, Texas. He became a farmer, and while looking after his farm and providing for his little household, he applied himself diligently to the study of law at night, and at all leisure intervals, and by continuing this dual occupation, was qualified and admitted to the bar in March, 1887. He at once began practice at Coldspring in San Jacinto County, and was a member of the bar there until 1903. Since then he has had his home and practice in Houston, and became associated with the law firm of Hume, Robinson, and Hume. His partnership continued until April 1, 1910, when Governor Campbell appointed him judge of the criminal district court of Harris County to fill the unexpired term of Judge Ed. R. Campbell. Such was his record on the bench during those two years, that in 1912 he was chosen at the regular election for the term of four years. Judge Robinson enjoys a reputation for broad learning and absolute impartiality as a judge, and is held in high esteem by all the members of the Harris County bar.

Fraternally he is a Master Mason, and belongs to the Knights of Honor, the Knights and Ladies of Honor, the Woodmen of the World, the Lodge no. 151 of Houston Elks, the Loyal Order of Moose, and the Houston Turn Verein.

At Galveston in 1882, Judge Robinson married Miss Annie Bell Dorroh, daughter of Dr. John Dorroh of Mississippi. Her mother was a descendent of Caesar Rodney, who was **one of the signers of the Declaration of Independence.'**

Governor Wood's House

Barb then turned to Bess and asked, " What can you tell us about **Governor George Tyler Wood**'s house?" Bess replied, "Well, it was a beautiful house. It had a huge fireplace that opened up into the living room, and to the front bedroom on the other side." Barb then asked,

"Did you see it, or just hear about it?" Bess continued, "I stayed there for awhile. I loved it!" Barb asked, "What about the house nearby, where the Mcgowens lived, and today is the Logan's house. When was it built?" Bill interjected, " That's the mystery. No one can figure out when that house was built. That's the big mystery." Barb turned to Bess and asked, "Well, it was Dr. McGowen who lived there, isn't that right?" Bess explained, "Dr. MeGowen had married Henry's daughter, Jessie, and so Dr. McGowen built the house of which you speak on Henry's daughter's land. Today, it's the Logan's house."

Gilbert, Eliza Jane, and General Lafayette

Bill turned toward Barb, and said, "You asked about Gilbert. Gib, who came to Texas with his two brothers, Robert Tod and Henry, had graduated with honors at the University of North Carolina in 1851, and was a member of the Philanthropic Society at the university. He was named after the French General Gilbert Du Motier Marquis de Lafayette. Gib's name is Gilbert De Motier Robinson. Lafayette is the General who helped the Americans defeat the British in the American Revolutionary War. It was Gib's mother, Eliza Jane, who danced with the famous General when she was seventeen. Her father, Robert, had been a close friend and ally of the General."

General Gilbert Due Motier Marquis De Lafayette

As my mind slipped for a moment into the past, I could only imagine the way it must have been in Montgomery, Alabama, that evening at the Ball held in the General's honor in 1824. **President James Monroe** had invited Lafayette to be the 'nation's guest', as a Thank You gesture for his contribution to the military victory of the Amenican Revolution.

> May I have the honor of this dance, Mademoiselle?", the great General asked. Bowing and extending his white gloved hand, wearing all the regalia of a French military officer, he reached for Eliza Jane. Blushing in her lace lined southern dress, the young, beautiful lady gracefully accepted his offer, and said, "Thank you, General."

Returning to our conversation about Gilbert, Bill continued, "Gilbert was very smart, but he was not very energetic. All he wanted to do was read. He was an avid reader, and he didn't do much else. But when the War started, he goes back to Alabama, to Lownesboro, and joins an infantry regiment there that was formed in Montgomery, and his regiment then served under the command of **General Stonewall Jackson.** He survives the War, and comes back to Point Blank. Then, one evening, in the late 1860s, the Robinson boys were sitting on your front porch when they saw the sky light up over toward Gib's place. So they get on their horses, and ride toward the fire. Sure enough, Gilbert's house was engulfed in a wall of flames, but Gib was just sitting there on a stump, reading a book. The brothers asked, 'Why are you just sitting there reading a book? Why aren't you trying to put out the fire?' Gib smiled and responded,'What can I do about it?', and went on reading."

Young William

"Young William, Jr. had come out to visit his brothers a little later, but before the Civil War started," Bill continued. "This was about 1859. In 1861, the Civil War broke out. William goes down to Coldspring and joins the 'Polk County Grays.' The Polk County Grays become a part of Hood's Texas Brigade. Hood's Brigade become a famous Confederate unit. He fights all the way through the war, until the 'Battle of the Wilderness.' The yankees were breaking through, and the battle was looking bleak. But **General Lee** was there, and the Texas Brigade was there. General Lee, somewhat at indecision as what to do, was suddenly approached by a group of soldiers. Lee asked, 'Who are you?' Shouting voices said, 'We are the Texans. We are Hood's brigrade!' Lee responded,' I can always count on my Texans.' With a renewed confidence, Lee rode to the front to sound the charge, but then a Texas sargent grabbed the reins of Lee's famous horse, Traveller, and said, 'We're not going anywhere until you move to the rear.' So the Texans sound the charge and stop the Yankees, but in the victory, young William is killed."

Barb and I thanked our gracious hosts, and left Houston for Point Blank with a greater appreciation for the historical significance of our plantation, and for the emotional feeling you get when you dig something out of the ground that was once an important part of peoples lives so long ago. Bess and Bill, through their memories, and in their own way, were helping the plantation to live once again.

Chapter 11

Triumph and Tradgedy

Tod Sr., Tod Jr. & Mary D

Carving the wilderness to their needs, sacrificial to the elements, and fighting sickness and disease, the courageous Robinson family struggled to make their plantation a prosperous venture into a new land. In 1857, who would have thought that soon there would be a terrible war that would change their lives forever. After the war, the real struggle began. The artifacts we have found bear witness to a time of hard labor, and tribulation. By 1879, when Robert Tod died, he had given his all and had done his best, but the plantation was over $20,000.00 in debt.

But then, a champion of the Robinson family would emerge. Tod, Sr. took over his father's estate. A sharp and shrewd businessman, builder, entrepaneur, and dedicated husband and father, Tod Sr. would pay off his father's debts within two years, and bring the plantation to it's greatest glory, and accomplish all this, almost completely blind. He had lost most of his sight as a teenager while on a hunting trip. Banker, mercantile businessman, and cotton exporter, Tod Sr.'s intelligent descions would make the Robinson Plantation the envy of the Trinity River cotton exporters. At a time when the wheels of the industrial revolution made goods and services available to the west, Tod Sr. took full advantage of this opportunity to make the plantation a very prosperous enterprise. Many of the artifacts we have found come from this era. In 1884, Tod Sr. applied for the first post office in Point Blank, and became the first postmaster.

Tod, Sr.
master of the plantation
circa 1925

Ora Lee McClanahan Robinson
holding Libby Robinson
1917

In the meantime, Tod Jr., one of his father's four children married a young lady known as Mary D. Gordon. Mary D. was very active in social affairs, and in politics. As Bill had explained, "The democratic party flew a plane into Point Blank to pick her up and take her as a guest to the Democratic National Convention. In May of 1929, in a full-page article on Mary D., the 'East Texas' magazine wrote:

> If further evidence of the progressiveness of San Jacinto County is desired, consider the fact that its county wide chamber of commerce has as its president not a double-fisted businessman, but a charming member of the fair sex, Mrs. Mary D. Robinson of Point Blank. She is county councillor of the East Texas Chamber of Commerce. Mrs. Robinson is a member of the family of Robinsons mentioned as having lived in the vicinity for four generations, and in that section, the people will tell you that Mrs. Robinson is the biggest factor in San Jacinto County's surge forward.

Mary D. Robinson
1930, Huntsville, Texas

In going through some of Libby's old photos and clippings, I also found an invitation addressed to Mary D., postmarked, May 27, 1939. It read:

> You are cordially invited to be a member of The Honorary Reception Committee to greet **Mrs. Franklin D. Roosevelt** at her lecture, Tuesday evening, March fourteenth, nineteen thirty-nine at eight o'clock in the Music Hall in Houston.

Also, Mary D. had a beautiful singing voice. She was invited to sing at many special occasions. One clipping from the 'Huntsville Item' newspaper read:

> Mrs. Mary D. Robinson of Point Blank acccompanied on the piano by Mrs. Calloway of Oakhurst, sang two beautiful solos. After the solos, Congressman Upshaw requested Mrs.

Robinson to sing at his meeting that night at the Methodist Church. She accepted the invitation to sing.

A photo, dated 1930, shows Mary D. at a fox hunt in Huntsville, sitting on the horse 'Bozo', given to her by the Texas Department of Corrections Director, Lee Simmons. She is dressed in all the English regalia that fox hunters wear.

By the late 1920s however, the tide had already begun to turn toward an ominous ending of the wealth of the Robinson plantation. As Bill had explained, " Mary D. had opened a clothing store, Tod Sr, owned a general store, and Tod Jr. (Little Tod), kept the books for both stores. Tod, Sr also had several other businesses. Then, in 1927, Tod Sr. died, and Little Tod was challenged to attend to his father's finances. The plantation was getting deep in debt, the great depression set in , prohibition was enforced, which shut down Tod, Sr.'s saloon, and Little Tod died pre-maturely. The day of reckoning was at hand. It was 1931! The stock market crashed. The debt collectors would take much of the Robinson land , and the businesses would go bankrupt. The plantation would never recover. As Bill had explained, " The creditors, while they took much of the land, could not get all of it because Ora Lee Robinson, Tod Sr.'s wife had given some of the land to relatives, and some of it was protected as homestead land. They were going to take **your house** also, but Aubrey Hugh, Tod Jr.'s brother, stepped in and hired a lawyer, and won a court battle. Thus, the plantation house remained in the Robinson family, but the large 3500 acre plantation was gone forever."

Aubrey Hugh and Jessie Robinson
circa 1915

Chapter 12

The Last Descendent

Elizabeth (Libby) Hansen Robinson 1916-2007

When we made the move from Arizona in 78, Barbara's mother, Velma Duncan came with us. Over the years, she and Libby became the best of friends. Velma had always been a history buff. In 1995 she suggested that we sit down with Libby and let her tell us about the history of the plantation as she remembered it. After all, it had been her home most of her life. She was the last of the Robinson descendents to live in the house. Completely oblivious to the fact that I would use the video tape later to write a book, we sat down with her as she shared her memories of the Robinson plantation. Libby explained that both she and her brother, Hugh Tod, were born in the living room. In those days, the living room was often used as a bedroom. It was easier to keep warm than the upstairs, and easier to take care of the sick, and the bedridden. She said the house had four 20x20 rooms with a foyer upstairs, and a 'dog run' down below. Barb asked her, "We have heard there is a cellar buried outside next to the house. Is that true?" Libby responded, "Yes, according to an elderly 'Negra' woman who lived there as a slave, it was a clay cellar, and it was at the south corner of the house next to the back porch." Negra was a term used by Southerners in a respectful way to refer to black people. Libby continued, "They filled it in in the early 1900s." Barb commented, "I wonder if there is anything still in it." Libby answered, "It's possible. They say old man

Robert Tod used to store his whiskey there, or there may be confederate money buried there."

"What other stories have you heard about Robert Tod?," I asked. Libby responded, "Shortly after Robert Tod had the plantation house built, the man who built it decided he wanted the house. He tried to get 'Bob' to sell it to him, but when Robert Tod turned him down, the man tried to scare him and his wife, Mary, out of the house. They began to hear strange noises from the thick woods all around them, and from noises on top of the house, especially at night. The builder tried to make the Robinsons believe the place was haunted. He would hang dead animals from trees, and hide in the forest making moaning sounds like a crying woman. But those Robinson boys, Robert Tod, Henry, and Gilbert set a trap. They hid out in the woods one night and waited for a sound to come from between them and the house. Sure enough, near midnight, they heard crying, moaning sounds. They caught the builder red handed, and made him apologize to the family members that he had scared to death."

Libby continued with her stories, " There was the time when Granddaddy (Tod Sr.) made his two boys, Tod Jr. and Aubrey Hugh, chop wood everyday for two weeks. You see, at the corner of the house near the rear balcony, there was a big oak tree. Deep into the night, the boys would go out onto the balcony, climb down the tree, and ride their horses all night. Some say they were meeting girls down at the creek. Whatever the reason, Tod Sr. noticed that his work horses seemed very tired, again and again. When he questioned the boys, they 'fessed up', but Hugh said, 'Well Pa, we were just having fun!' So their father responded, 'Well boys, now you can have fun chopping wood for two weeks.'

"Libby, what is that big book you have there?, I asked. Libby replied, "That's Grandaddy's ledger. He owned a mercantile store——a general store. That's what he kept record of all his business transactions in." We opened the ledger. It was heavy, and about three inches thick. The date was 1914, right at the height of the glory days of the Robinson plantation. There were familiar names in there of families we have known in Point Blank, such as the Hopkins, Trapp, and Travis. It was a record of what they bought, and how much it cost. For example, bacon at 25 cents, lard at 15 cents, and snuff at 10 cents."

"What is this little book you have here, Libby?," I asked. "Oh, that's my teacher's grade book. Her name was Mrs. Thompson. Her family gave it to me when she passed." The book had written on the front cover,'Texas

Teacher's Daily Register, 1921-22, Point Blank, Texas. Inside were all the students grades, including Libby's and Bess's. Libby was five years old, and in the first grade. Bess was seven, and in the 2nd grade. They both made straight 'A's. Other children's names listed were Bitsy Robinson 8, Rennie Owens 11, Pearl Currie 13, Virginia Counts 7, Modine Groom 11, Pink Blanks 7, Codine Groom 8, Holly Blanks 5, Ethel Adams 8, Annie Counts 14, Hettie Groom14, Vivian Grant 11, Ted Walker 15, Demetry Walker 12, Fisher Owens 11, Bruce Owens 9, Oscar Owens 7, Justice Counts 12, Ed Counts 10, John Adams 11, Ervin Adams 10, Charlie Counts 16, Kit Walker 17, Lee Grant 7, and Jim Grant 13. As you can see, Mrs. Thompson had her work cut out for her, with twenty-seven students in a one room school house (the church), ranging from ages 5 to 17. Her salary was also listed: $100.00 per month, and $800.00 per year. A quote from a page on the ''Maximum Salaries for Teachers in 1921, read, 'A teacher holding a permanent state certificate shall not receive wages in excess of $150.00 per month. A teacher teaching first grade shall not receive more than $125.00 per month, and a teacher holding a 2nd grade certificate shall not receive more than $100.00 per month."

A typical day at school in the little country town of Point Blank would have begun exactly like this:

"Children, stand, and repeat after me."
''Our Father, who art in Heaven, hallowed be thy name.
Thy kingdom come, Thy will be done,
On earth as it is in Heaven.
Give us this day our daily bread,
And forgive us our debts, as we forgive our
debtors.
And lead us not into temptation,
But deliver us from evil,
For thine is the kingdom, and the power, and the glory,
Forever, Amen!

Following this Christian prayer, the children would remain standing, with hands over their hearts, to recite the following words:

I pledge allegiance to the flag of the United States of America, and to the Republic for which it stands, one nation under God, indivisible, with liberty and justice for all.

Celebrating Christmas and Easter was the traditional and natural thing to do, with programs always performed reflecting these historical events. Discipline for disruptive behavior was swift, final, and effective, and support from the parents was close to 100%. The children were taught that they lived in a Christian nation, blessed by God. They were also taught that the United States is the greatest, most powerful country in the world, and that Texas is the greatest state in those United States. As I continued thumbing through the register, I could not help but notice the *'Instructions for display of the American flag*:

> That it is the wish of the people of Texas, through their Representatives in the Texas Legislature, that the State Superintendent of Public Instruction shall include, in instructions to city and county superintendents, provisions requiring the flag of each schoolhouse to be kept indoors, to be displayed on the exterior of the building only in good and fair weather, on suitable occasions, and at such regular intervals as may be desirable, at the same time providing such **regular use of the flag in patriotic exercises as may inspire the children of the State of Texas the proper reverence and enthusiasm for the Star Spangled Banner of the greatest Republic in the world.** Austin, Texas, September 1st, 1921.

Asking Libby yet another question, Barb inquired, "Didn't you serve as postmaster for awhile?" Libby answered, "No, but my husband, Rudolph was postmaster from 1953 to 1966. You see, Grandaddy was the first postmaster from 1884 to 1914, and then his daughter held the position until 1949."

State *Historical* Landmark

Barb then inquired, "When was the State Historical Marker awarded to the plantation, Libby? Was there a ceremony, and who was there? Libby replied, "The plaque was placed in the front yard in 1975 by the Texas Historical Comission. It was within the last three years that the plantation would belong to the Robinson family. Several of our relatives were there, and Bill Blythe, who was then a state representative, gave a speech on the history of the plantation. It was a very special occasion." Libby passed away in 2007, living to see a time of more changes in the world, than in the previous several hundred years put together. She was buried in the Robinson cemetary in Point Blank.

Chapter 13

Jessie Mae Polk (Howard),(1916-)

Childhood Friends

As the summer of 2010 came to a close, I was ever aware and searching for clues to, and evidence for the long drama that permeated the Robinson family. School had begun, and I was driving home on one hot August afternoon. As I approached our driveway, I noticed the County Constable, Alvin Wyatt, sitting in his patrol car across the highway from our home. We had met at the San Jacinto County Historical Commission auction earlier that month down in Camilla. So I stopped to say hello. We talked about the auction, and about county politics coming up in November, and then again in May. I asked him if I had told him about finding the artifacts, and the resulting developments of the past year. I enjoy sharing it so much with others, that I am seldom sure whether I have already told it to the person I'm talking to. He said, "No, you haven't." So I told him all about the discoveries, and the research I've been gathering on the Robinson family, including the taped interview with Bess and Bill Blythe Robinson. Alvin then suggested, You know, Mr. West, you ought to go and talk to Jessie Mae Polk (Howard). She is 93 years old, and was Bess's childhood playmate." "Well, where does she live?", I asked. "Right around the corner from you,' Alvin answered. I was excited, to say the least, to be able to talk to another living witness to the glory days of the plantation, and this time from the black perspective. On the same afternoon, I dropped in to see a 93 year old neighbor I had never met.

Friendly and very acommodating, I was given a warm welcome into the home of Jessie Mae and her daughter 'Pinkey.' I was surprised to find this beautiful southern lady was healthy, spirited, and very sharp and sound of mind. I told her my story. I shared with her that I had found in Libby's old photographs a picture of a black lady, whose name Bill Blythe had told me was Georgie Mae Adams, affectionately known as 'Dog Gone.' I asked Jessie, 'Did you know Dog Gone?' Jessie responded, ''I sure did. She was my Grandma. She was the cook at the 'big house,' and the daughter of a slave.'' I asked Jessie if I could return in a couple of days and videotape a conversation with her. She said that would be just fine.

Jessie Mae Polk
2010

Georgie Mae Adams
"Dog Gone"
1920

I returned on the said day with my camera, and she dug deep into her past to tell of some dramatic and fascinating times. She was dressed in her Sunday's best, looking her prettiest in a purple dress decorated with floral print. We sat down and I spoke, "Jessie Mae, thank you for letting me come over and ask you a few questions" She responded, "I'm just very delighted to have you here." I asked my first question, "Do you remember what the old town of Point Blank looked like when you were very young. What kind of stores were here and where were they located?" Jessie responded, "Yes, I do. There was one main store. I guess they called it a merchandise, or general store.That was the Robinson's store. You know where they park those big trucks sometimes close to the caution light. That's where it was located, and I was raised up just below those big cedar trees that grow there. Our house was just on the other side of the store. Me and the Robinson 'chirrens' played all around that store. So I called Miss Ora Lee 'Grandma', and I called Mr. Robinson 'Grandpa.' I thought it was the right and natural thing to do, but my Mama told me to stop doing that, 'It wasn't proper.' But then, Miss Ora Lee stepped in and said, You let that girl call us Grandma and Grandpa any time she wants. She's just like one of mine. The Robinsons treated us very well. Well, I was raised up there, but I was born over there across from Libby's house, behind where Greg Magee's office is. We lived next to the 'big house. " The big house was, of course, the house Bess was raised in, constructed by her father, Tod Sr.. However, it had been built too close to the river bottom. When the mighty Trinity was dammed up in 1969 at Camilla, the developers who built Governor's Point subdivision disassembled the beautiful home which Bess had been raised in.

I continued with the questions, "Jessie Mae, you mentioned the mercantile store, but what other kinds of buildings were there?" Jessie answered, "There was a Masonic Hall, or a 'Woodmen of the World' lodge. There was also the Robinson's church, and a saloon." "Where was the church located,' I asked. 'Was it the same church that's located at the Robinson Cemetary now?" Jessie Mae replied, "No, that's not the same church. You know the Horton church which sits up on a hill about three miles south of Point Blank? That's the church. It was located on the left going toward the Robinson Cemetary. They moved to the new location years ago." What do you remember about playing with Bess and Libby when you were children?," I continued. Jessie Mae grinned and replied, "Well, we played together all the time, and fought together.We were mean at times, but we had a good time most of the time. But I just loved them, and I think they felt the same way. I remember when Libby was about 12, and had a serious injury to her back. I helped take care of her until she was well."

"OK, Jess, you were born after the slave era, but you must have known some of your people who had been slaves. Is that right, I asked. "I don't remember much concerning the slaves, but you know the house you bought was a slave house. I do know that Fannie Mae Hopkins who took care of Libby in that house, was the granddaughter of Sally Hopkins, who had been a slave. Fannie Mae's mother was Thelma. She also had a brother they called 'Goat', but his real name was Lewis Walker. Everybody had a nickname in those days." I asked Jessie, "What did they call you?" She answered "Tootsie! I have a picture of Libby's dad, Aubrey Hugh, which I will show you. They called him 'Boy'. I remembered as Jessie Mae told me this, that when we first bought our place, our nearest neighbors, the Walkers, had several children, mostly boys, all with nicknames. There was Bird, Rocky, Rod, and Funky Joe. It wasn't long after we were there that they gave my son and I nicknames also. As I recall, I was Willie, and Vince, because of a growth spurt, was called Weed. So the tradition continued.

"Any special memories between you and Bess, and Libby?, I asked. Jessie replied, " I remember Bess had something wrong with her back when she was a young girl. I don't know if she had surgery or what. Her parents wouldn't let her get far from the house while she was healing up, so I went over and played with her all the time. You see, my mother worked there at the store for the Robinsons." I continued, "Jessie, for you in your long life, what were the best of times, and the worst of times?" Jessie answered, "Well, my Dad passed when I was about five years old. At that time, my mother and my grandma did domestic work for the Robinsons. Us 'chirren's' had to work in the fields. Believe it or not, these were some of the best times for me, because when all of us kids were choppin' cotton, we also played a lot too. But when times got really hard was during the depression when we didn't have much to eat, and many of my friends moved away. The men would hunt and bring home deer and small game for us to eat, and the women would raise as much food in the garden as they could.

'Gone With the Wind'

I reminded Jessie, "Speaking of the depression years, and hard times, Jessie, it was 1931 that the golden age of the plantation came to an end. Tod, Sr. had passed in 1927, Little Tod passed away in 1931, the plantation was deep in debt, the stock market crashed, and the depression years set in. Also, prohibition was enforced, which put the Robinsons saloon out of business. The debt collectors came, and much of the land was sold or given away. The great 3500 acre Robinson plantation was gone forever.

Jessie continued, "I also remember that Tod, Jr. and Mary D. had a nice car called a Georgie straight-eight. Do you remember a car called a Georgie straight-eight? I think it was a Pontiac. Before Tod Jr. died, he would always drive around the store at night, waving his lantern, I guess, for security reasons. We would sit on the front porch and just watch him drive round and round, with his lights on. Well, about two weeks after he passed away, we were sitting out there at night just like we always did. Suddenly, we saw car lights. It was little Tod's car, just going round and round the store,and the lantern was waving, but with no driver, and no one was waving the lantern. It was just swinging back and forth. Mary D. had gone into Huntsville, so we knew it couldn't be her. "Now wait a minute, Jessie Mae, you're telling me this was after he died?, I asked. She said, "Yes, we were sitting on the porch, and we actually saw this. We didn't see him personally, but, as God is my witness, we saw the car and the lantern just as sure as I'm looking at you. I remember making the remark to my sisters that it had to be Tod Jr. It's just like if I saw your truck driving around with nobody in it, I would have to assume that it was you driving it. We 'chirren' got scared and ran into the house. God knows I'm telling you the truth. I saw it with my own eyes."

Jesse continued, "You know, there was a large grocery chain in Houston. I think they're the ones who came and took just about everything. Little Tod would order truckloads of food and other items from them, on credit. Tod Sr. had bought a truck, and Little Tod would send my uncle, Sam Adams down to Houston to pick up the groceries, and whatever else they needed.

I'll tell you what else I remember, Jessie continued. You know, Little Tod kept the books, and many times when the store was closed on Sunday nights, us 'chirren' would walk home right alongside the store coming from church, and we could hear him get angry and slam that big thick book down on his desk, and voice his frustrations in a low undertone manner. We would stop and peek through the window and watch him vent his anger." I commented to Jessie, You know, Libby had one of those ledgers years ago, dated 1914. It was about three inches thick." Jessie Mae continued, " Well, one night, after he had died, we were walking home from church right down the alley by the store. There was a low light inside the building, and just as we walked by the same window, we heard that book slamming loudly down on Little Tod's desk. It went 'booom!!', just as sure as I'm sittin' here. We didn't stop that time.We ran straight home. We all heard it, every last one of us. There was a bunch of us 'chirren'. And he was gone. I mean he was deceased! This is **after** he died."

Responding to Jessie, I said, " You know, at one time, the Robinsons owned all of the land from snow hill all the way to the big bridge along the river. It must have been a devastating loss. But the Robinsons were a very generous family. You know that subdivision between here and the big bridge, called Point Lookout Estates? Tod Sr. gave that land to his daughter, Fannie Rose, for a wedding present. Can you imagine?" Jessie responded, "Mary D. gave the land to us where our church is built. You know, Liberty Baptist Church, down on Counts road. The debt collectors took it away from us, but then, we were able to buy it back a little later. And my Mama bought this land that this house is on from Mrs. Robinson (Ora Lee).

I turned to Jessie's daughter, Pinkey Polk, and asked, "Pinkey, is there anything you would like to ask your Mom before we stop the camera?" She replied, "Mother what do you remember about the railroads that came close to Point Blank?" Jessie reaffirmed what Bill Blythe had told me, "They would bring heavy equipment to Dodge from Houston, and then from Dodge, they would transport it to Oakhurst. If it was something to be delivered to Point Blank, they would move it on a thing you called a tram track, across the Snow Hill ridge toward Coldspring. They could get fairly close to Point Blank, and bring it here by way of oxen and mules."

I continued questioning Jessie, "You know, Jessie, behind our house is where we have found the majority of the artifacts---glassware, housewares, tools, weapons, et cetera. What do you remember about the area behind our house? Do you remember how many houses there were?" Jessie looked up, closed her eyes, and journeyed deep into the past, "One, two, three, four---I remember four. George Jones lived in one, Harrison Bass and his family lived in another, then there was Henry Harrison and Jack McKinney, and their families. That's four. That's all I can remember." "Well, Jessie,' I asked, 'maybe you can help me with this question. When you go behind the house with the metal detector and find an array and assortment of items, you can't say, 'Well, the kitchen was over here because of the silver ware, or the bedroom was over there because of the bed frames, or personal items. No sir, the items are scattered like they were hit by a giant wind. So, what happened, Jessie Mae? Did someone come in there and wipe those houses out with a caterpillar, or were they abandoned during the depression, and then a hurricane did the rest. What happened, Jessie Mae?" "I'll tell you what happened,' Jessie replied. ' All those people died one by one, and no one replaced them in the house. The younger people moved away. The houses and the items were left to the disgression of the others. When the plantation house was abandoned, people just came in and helped themselves. Eventually, the houses were torn down. Many of the items ended up on the ground. At one time, the plantation was in a state of decay, and destruction. You see, those houses were what we called the quarters.(slave quarters) There was a lot of activity there right behind your house."

"Do you have any photos of early Point Blank," I asked. Jessie replied, "No, but I have one of Aubrey Hugh Robinson, Libby's dad. I used to have photos of the entire Robinson family, but I gave them to Mary D."

Fannie May Hopkins babysitting
Libby Robinson - 1916

In parting, I said, "Thank you so much, Jessie Mae and Pinkey, for letting me come over and share these memories with both of you. This has been absolutely wonderful. My only regret is that I've waited 32 years to meet one of my very best neighbors."

Chapter 14

September, 2010

'I'm sorry, Aunt Lillie'

The pain from someone pinching and twisting my ear meant I had no choice, but to get up from the table and follow my Mamma, Hazel West, right out of the house. She demanded, "You get right back in there and apologize to your Aunt Lillie. You tell her you're sorry for asking for iced tea, or I'm gonna' whup yore bottom good. She's doing the best she can to put a meal on the table, and here you are complainin' that you don't have iced tea. She doesn't even have any ice. Now, hurry up!" "Yes, Ma'am," I replied. So back in the house I went, and said, "I'm sorry Aunt Lillie for asking for iced tea. Thank you for the water." She graciously accepted my apology. I sat down, ate my fried chicken and peas, drank my glass of water, and kept my mouth shut.

It was 1948, and I was eight years old. We had left Houston to visit my Uncle Ivan and Aunt Lillie Jones, and my seven cousins, whom I had never met, in a little town called Point Blank, Texas. At the time, I didn't know the name of the town. All I knew was that they lived 'out in the country'. My brother, Roy Gene, and my sister, Shirley, and I were raised in Houston where we had all the modern conveniences. We were 'citified', spoiled rotten. But when we arrived at Aunt Lillie's, we found a large family of nine, living in a two room log house, without electricity, or running water, and just as happy as could be. They were as country as turnip greens. The kids were running around bare foot, and wearing raggedy clothes.

They lived deep in the woods off a dirt road called Sandy Lane, and were happy and excited to see us.

Aunt Lillie killed two chickens, while the kids picked peas out of the garden. In a couple of hours the home made table was set, complete with fried chicken, black-eyed peas, greens, and a glass of well water. In retrospect, it was probably one of the healthiest meals I have eaten.

We played down by the river that day, caught a few catfish, and got muddy. I also had my first painful encounter with a 'bull nettle'. The deep sting on a tender ankle can be severe. Showing concern, all my cousins gathered round me. I cried a little, actually a lot, but Aunt Lillie had an old time cure for it. She put baking soda on it, and the pain went away. In the evening, all the kids, including me, took turns taking a bath next to the well in a number 3 washtub, in ice cold well water.

I remembered that day like no other, probably because of the contrast in our lives, and because of the kindness, and generosity of a family just as poor as the dirt they lived on.

In September, 2010, I realized that I still have a cousin, Iva Cooper (Jones), who lives on the same homeplace in a modern home close to the old log house. She was one of the seven. She was the same age as my brother, Roy Gene, having been born during the 'depression'. So I went to pay my cousin a visit, and we sat down to talk about old memories, and what she remembered about the Robinson family and the plantation, which was close by.

Aunt Lillie Jones
Two room log house
photo taken 2010

After discussing, and laughing about the visit in 1948, I asked Iva, "I want you to dig deep into your memory and tell me just what it was really like growing up here on the little farm in Point Blank?" She replied, "Well, you will have to forgive my country accent. I guess I will always have it." In consolation, I told Iva, "Hey, at one time, all of us had that east Texas accent. It's something to be proud of, so don't apologize for it." Iva also gave me permission to reflect some of her accent on these pages. Iva began, "Well, it was hard. We raised 'everythang' we ate, except most of the meat, which Daddy and the brothers would hunt and kill in the woods. We had to walk from 'hyar' to Point Blank to 'ketch' the school bus, which was three miles, and then walk home in the evening." Interrupting, I asked, "Where did you go to school?" "Oakhurst,' she responded. 'When we walked those three miles home, then we had our chores to do, like choppin' and gittin' in wood, bringing it in for the wood stoves to stay warm, or for the cookstove so Mamma could fix a meal. We had to clean the soot off the kerosene lanterns, and fill them full, cause we didn't have no electricity." "Iva, tell me a little more about living in that log house," I requested. She explained, "Well, it kept us dry. It wasn't very well insulated though, so we had to sleep under a lot of quilts because it would get so cold in the winter. In the summer it was very hot inside and outside the house. We didn't know nothin' about fans, or air conditioning. There was no electricity back then." I mentioned to Iva, "You drew your water from a well, didn't you?" She answered, "Yes, we drew our water from a well, but when the well went dry, we had to carry it from a 'sprang' down under the hill. And also, we would have to wash our clothes at the 'sprang' in a wash tub, using a rub board down 'aire' under the hill." I continued, "I remember Uncle Ivan telling me that he caught lots of catfish out of the Trinity River." Iva replied, "Yes, ever 'wonst' in a while, we would all walk through these woods down to the river, which was about 3 miles away. We'd camp out and spend the night down 'air.' We took our coffee pot and skillet with us, and we'd 'ketch' some fish and cook em' right there by the river. We'd just cook out, and have a good time." Then, I asked Iva, "Was Uncle Ivan related to Isaac Jones, who's buried here in the Isaac Jones Cemetery?" Iva explained, " Yes, Isaac Jones was my daddy's great-great grandpa, and Jim Jones was my Daddy's grandpa. He's buried out here behind my house. That's who raised my dad, was Jim Jones. He fought in the Civil War." "Iva', what about those family rumors that Uncle Ivan used to boot leg a little whiskey every now and then?", I asked. Iva shook her head, and answered, "No, Daddy never did bootleg any whiskey. In fact,

Daddy never did 'drank' or nothin' when I was growing up. I 'heerd' he might have drank a little after I was growed up, but he never did bootleg any whiskey. Now, I had an uncle that did. That's all he ever done, was bootleg." "Did he have a still close by, Iva?", I asked. Iva explained, " Oh, yeah, he had a still back over here towards the Blalock place. He made whiskey, and stored it in the woods. He had a friend who rode a gray horse and peddled the whiskey up and down the road. My uncle made it, and his friend sold it."

"Iva, how well did you know the Robinsons, and did you ever go into the plantation house when you were growing up?", I asked. "No, I never had the opportunity to go into the house until you bought it, but I did know Libby and her husband very well. They used to run the store, and the post office in Point Blank. But I 'heered' Daddy talk a lot about Tod Robinson and Little Tod. They owned the same general store in Point Blank, and I understand from Daddy's account, when he was young, that Point Blank was a pretty rough little town back then, Point Blank was. I 'heered' that Little Tod, when his daddy died, he had lots of money, but then he went broke. " Iva grinned, and explained, "That was before I was even borned." I reaffirmed, "Me too!"

Iva Cooper Jones
2010

Hazel West 2010
Living at the plantation

Iva continued, "Well, like I said, it was rough growin' up, and times were hard. After I was about 13 or 14 years old, my brothers Sam and Billy Wayne and I used to cut pulp wood back over 'heer' in the woods to make a little money, you know. Daddy would pay the timber company 'stumpage', and then we would cut it and sell it, and make a little money. (1913 definition of 'stumpage'- fixed price for standing timber per tree, without the land.) Back then it was amazing what I could do, and I didn't weigh very much. We didn't have to worry about workin' out, because we always had somethin' to do. But I could chunk them 'pupwood' sticks up on them trucks just like them young boys. I grew up working very hard, I thought."

Before I left, I asked Iva whether she had any old photographs of Point Blank around the turn of the 20th century. She answered, "No, we didn't even have a camera." I've not been able to find any photos which date back to that time. Maybe it's because no one had a camera.

After taking a few photos of the old log house, I said goodbye and thank you to Iva, and left. As I drove away, I remembered the day we drove away from there in 1948. The same sweetness and kindness my cousins showed us that day, was still evident in my cousin, Iva.

On the way home, I decided to stop by the Isaac Jones Cemetery for the very first time, to pay respect to a distant family relative for the very first time. The cemetary was right on the edge of the Trinity River, and I was surprised to find that the only resident there was Isaac Jones. There was not even a stone monument, but there was a Texas Historical Marker. It read, "Isaac Jones (1793-1878):

Individualistic pioneer of Texas. Born in Mississippi, he moved here 1834, receiving Mexican land grant on West Bank of Trinity River. Served three months in army of Texas Republic, 1836-38. Operated ferry at Jones Bluff 1858-1861. Wife: Elizabeth (Martin).

September 10
In Pursuit of a State **Archeological** Landmark

Sandy looked me straight in the eye and said, "You don't write a book on archeology and history without a trip to the courthouse, Bill. You must research the deed records, the early roadmaps and the structure locations." She was on the land rich in artifacts behind our house making final preparations to send a package to Austin in quest of a State Archeological Landmark. I responded, "I've already made one trip to the courthouse in Coldspring, although I didn't find much." As I helped her stretch out the long tape, and find the corners of the designated area with the GPS locater, she explained, "The courthouse in Coldspring may not go far enough back. Remember, Point Blank was first in Liberty County. So, go to the Library in Liberty. It's a very good one." I would soon make a day long trip to Liberty. My digging had already shifted from the ground to the literature and memories of the Robinson family and plantation.

Isaac Jones
1793-1878

September 11
A Birthday Celebration

Today, while a nation mourned, and searched for the healing of its wounds, Barb and I attended a birthday celebration no less American and patriotic. Jessie Mae turned 94 years young. Bill Blythe and his mother, Bess, had called her that morning from Houston to wish her a grand day. She had no photos of her grandmother, Georgie Mae Adams, aka 'Dog gone,' but I did. 'Dog Gone' had worked as a cook at the 'big house' in Point Blank. I made a copy of the photo and enlarged it to an 8x10, and gave it to her. In her gracious southern way, she showed much gratitude and appreciation. Friends and family came from miles around to celebrate this special life. When I asked her how she was doing, her answer was, "I am blessed."

September 13
Tour & Presentation To The
San Jacinto County Historical Commission

The discovery of the artifacts continued having resonating effects for bringing the plantation back to life. More people were becoming aware of a place in the county where a prominent family struggled, endured, and thrived for 120 years, and that artifacts had been discovered recently which represented that long span of time.

The Historical Commission requested a tour and presentation following the September monthly meeting. The meeting would be held across the highway from the plantation at Greg Magee's law office. My son, Vince & I attended the meeting, which was Chaired by Betty Magee. The agenda included:

1. Welcome members and visitors
2. Committee reports and appointment of committee chairs and members.
3. Old and new business: consideration, discussion, and possible votes concerning the scheduling of upcoming year's events and fund raisers, to include but not limited to :

1) Celebration of San Jacinto County—140 years
2) Halloween activities on the grounds of the old jail museum
3) Trade Days
4) Business part of meeting adjourned, followed by a presentation by Bill West at the Robinson plantation.

We enjoyed attending the meeting, and I felt honored for two reasons: one, to be asked to address the Commission, and two, to be the one who would speak for the Robinson family.

The tour was much like the the others I have made, first the museum, and secondly, the house. Each time I make a presentation, there is more that I have in artifacts and historical knowledge to share with those who are on the tour. I enjoy sharing the plantation immensely, but this particular group was special. They were all historically minded, and thus, took the time to read, study, and ask questions about the house and the artifacts. Some even had stories of their own about their families and their land.

After touring the house, Barbara had prepared snacks and goodies, and drinks for all to enjoy. It was mainly then that I begin to hear historical stories about the families of members of the Historical Commission. It was a splendid evening.

Vince and I are looking forward to more involvement in the Historical Commission, hoping one day that we might become members, and help preserve the rich history of San Jacinto County, as well as continuing to pump life back into the once neglected and abandoned Robinson plantation house, and reviving the memory of the Robinson family in Point Blank, Texas.

September 18
Discovery of the 1924 Indian Head Nickel

"Hey, Son, would you like to go out and do a little digging?" Vince replied, "Sure, Dad!" Barbara had bought four Live Oak trees, and was getting ready to plant them in front of the house on the outside of the pickett fence. Four big holes had been dug for the trees. "Let's go hear what the metal detector has to say, before she fills the holes back in," I continued. So, we took the detector out there and began to search. It wasn't long before I got a consistent signal, and then a bell ringer. We dug about five inches down, and there it was---a 1924 Indian Head nickel, with a buffalo on the back. I thought to myself, "That fits, this coin could have easily been dropped during the golden years of the plantation, which was 1880-1927." Who might have dropped the coin? The only thing we do know is that coins were more plentiful at the Robinson house during the golden age.

September 22
Discovery of Toy Pistol

"Bill, would you like to check this pile of dirt with the metal detector before I fill the hole back in?", Barbara asked. "Yes, I'll check this hole while you're digging the next hole", I answered. Barb was on the third hole for the four oak trees she was planting in front of the house. While I was checking one hole, she was digging the other. I know, it sounds like it should have been the other way around. I should have been digging while she was doing the searching. But I did have an ailing back, and that's the truth.

Suddenly, she said, pulling her shovel out of the ground, "Uh Oh! I have found either a piece of pipe, or a pistol. It turned out to be the latter. Buried 12" deep, the object was heavily encrusted with rust and dirt. It was hardly recognizable, but a few minutes on the wire brush wheel left little doubt that it was a small handgun, carried in the pocket, or in someone's boot. Disappointment would come when I found out on the internet that it was not a real gun at all. It was a cast iron toy cap gun made by Zip Hubley Cast Iron Toys, 1930.

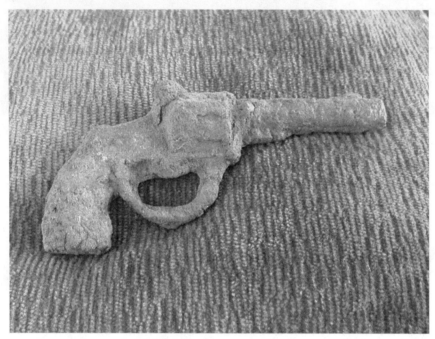

Hubley made toy pistol 1930

Chapter 15

Theories

The Magneto

Is it possible that the magneto we have found is off of Aubrey Hugh's 1913 Model T Ford Roadster? A magneto is part of the car's ignition system. According to an article written in the book, <u>San Jacinto County</u> in 1994, it very well could be:

First Model T in San Jacinto County Recalled

It has been said, when Henry Ford built the Model T car, he put America on wheels," said Arnett Jones, Sr. (Grandson of Isaac Jones). It was 80 years ago when Ford's Model T came to the little farming community of Point Blank, Texas. Tod Robinson Sr., a wealthy land owner, merchant, and farmer, bought his son Hugh Robinson, a 1913 Model T Ford Roadster. Hugh was Libby Robinson's father.

"Hugh's Roadster was a beauty, "remarked Arnett Jones, Sr. "It was of a dark color, trimmed in brass with a brass radiator. At the back was a small gasoline tank and a tool box that held the car crank, pliers, jack, and a pump to pump up the small tires. The Roadster was equipped with carbide lights, a rubber horn stood out from the steering wheel to blow if anything was in the way. The horn was not used much, for when the stock heard the "gasoline wagon" coming, they headed for the woods to hide. The Roadster had a tarpaulin top that folded to the back to have air conditioning. After the key was turned on, the crank was inserted in the front near the bottom of the Model T. The crank was turned around and around, being careful not to let the crank 'kick' you. After the engine was started, Hugh was ready to travel. When the engine was hard to start, Hugh learned to jack up one of the back wheels before starting to crank the Roadster...

It was a busy day at the Tod Robinson store that Saturday. The farmers came from near and far to get their mail and buy their groceries on credit. They paid Tod in the fall when they sold their cotton. Hugh was late coming to help Tod. "Why don't Boy, as Tod called Hugh, come and help me?" All at once it sounded like a tornado hit outside, " What in the blankety-blank is going on?," asked Tod. "It's Hugh driving up in his Model T Roadster, causing the oxen, mules, and horses to stampede, tearing the wagons, carts, and buggies up," said one of the farmers. "Tell that blankety-blank Boy to get that blankety-blank model T away from here before he runs all of my business away. "I'll have my blacksmith to repair the damage." From then on, Hugh came to work in the store and post office in a buggy pulled by a large sorrel horse. Hugh bought gasoline in Oakhurst for his Model T, for there was none to buy in Point Blank."

And -------What about that large sorrel horse? Could one of the large bits that we have dug up be the one used on that horse? Maybe! It certainly is a possibility.

The Heart-Shaped Pendant

Is it possible that the blue heart-shaped pendant that we excavated belonged to Libby Robinson? Well, maybe! In a photo that we have of Libby when she was about one year old, she is wearing a heart-shaped pendant, seemingly identical to the one we found.

The Blacksmith's Hammer

Is it possibile that we know the very name of the personal blacksmith for the Robinson family, and that he used the hammer that Vince and I dug up? Is he also the one who fashioned the home made spur that we found?

I found the following article in the yellow book of <u>San Jacinto County, A Glimpse into the Past</u>. It read:

> In the late afternoon, Arnett Jones, Sr. tied his meal to the saddle of his horse and rode up the hill to the Tod Robinson store. After buying sugar, coffee, flour, and a bottle of snuff from the clerk, he'd walk over to the Tod Robinson saloon to 'pick up' on some more news. "If I stayed long enough, I'd see several fist fights," he said, " and a number of drunks wobblying around on the street."

Just before dark, Arnett Sr. stuffed the bottle of snuff in his blue overall pocket, and mounted his horse for the ride home. He wouldn't be back until the next Saturday, unless a piece of machinery broke down and he had to come into the <u>blacksmith shop</u> during the week for repairs. <u>Isaac Owens</u> ran the blacksmith shop during the week for Tod Robinson. He ran the grist mill on Saturday, and the cotton gin in the fall. Tod gave Isaac two dollars a day for his work, and gave Ned Richardson, a Negro man, a quart of whiskey for helping Isaac.

Did the hammer we excavated belong to Isaac? Maybe so!

The Double-Edged Axes

Beneath the plantation house, one can see the huge, one foot square hewed out cypress timbers that supports the whole structure. The axe marks left by the slaves are plainly visible. The timbers are 'notched in', and held together will wooden pegs and square nails, interlocked throughout the foundation.

Is it possible that the three double-edged axes we have discovered are the very tools that did this work? Well, maybe part of the work. Logs in those days were commonly hewed with a much wider, single edge axe. However, these axes could have been used on smaller detailed work. The axes were found in different locations, but all were buried eight to ten inches deep. This depth is a strong indication that the axes are from the very first days. They were heavily corroded and rusted, and one was unusually large and heavy. This axe required a strong and muscular back. My back aches just thinking about it.

Padlocks: Sargent, Corbin, & Bohannen

Heavy padlocks are used when you have something valuable, and there are people around whom you do not trust. We have excavated five such padlocks. They were made by James Sargent Co., 1859, Corbin Russwin, 1882, and Wilson Bohannen Co., 1885. The Bohannen lock, made of solid brass, is in near perfect condition. The right key would probably open it. It has information imprinted on it which reads, "Wilson Bohannen, Brooklyn, New York, Patent date, May 26, 1885."

This time frame for the locks places them squarely in the hands of Tod, Sr. He probably inherited the Sargent padlocks from his father, Robert Tod, and then bought the Corbin and the Bohannen locks in addition. The time of Tod, Sr. was one of prosperity. He would need several padlocks in order to secure his most valued posessions. It is not only possible, but probable that these locks belonged to Tod, Sr.

Home Comfort Cookstove Shelf

Is it possible that Christmas morning, 1865, brought Mary McGowen Robinson, wife of Robert Tod, a brand new 'fleur de lis' style Home Comfort cookstove? Well, it is possible. The war was over, and the economy was beginning to move again. The plantation was still making money off of cotton exports, and the new home needed a cookstove. There was none nicer than the 'fleur de lis'. Internet research shows this woodstove was made in 1864, by the Wrought Iron Range Co., St. Louis, Missouri.

One of the first excavations we made was a shelf and a towel rack from this stove. Did it belong to Mary McGowen, whose family also owned a large plantation at Camilla? Maybe so!

Single Shot Shotgun

Was this shotgun a gift from Robert Tod to his son, Tod, Sr.? Maybe the gun, too, came on a Christmas morning in the 1870s. By 1878, the plantation had plunged to $20,000 dollars in debt. Maybe the love for his son outweighed his financial wisdom, and thus became part of the numbers in red.

Research has shown the gun to be made by Harrington & Richardson Firearms Co., 1871. Much of the food on the Robinson table, in the early days, was put there at the end of a shotgun barrel.

The Toy Pistol

Little boys and cowboy pistols have had a special bond since the days of the great Texas cattle drives in the 1870s. For a young boy to wake up on Christmas morning to a brand new shiney cap gun was exciting as getting a first puppy. Such a scenario could have happened to little Hugh Tod Robinson, Libby's little brother, on Christmas morning, 1931. He was eleven years old. The six shooter was a 'Zip Hubley' cast iron cap gun, made in 1930 in Lancaster, Pennsylvania.

One day, or perhaps one night, when the kids were playing 'cowboys and Indians' in the front yard, the gun was dropped. Maybe a sudden rainstorm drove the children into the house. The gun sank deeper into the soil, and thus remained encased in the ground for some seventy- plus years.

Only the lucky shovel of Barb planting an oak tree would give the pistol life once again, on September 22, 2010. The cap gun might have been one of the few highlights in Hugh's life, as an infection from a cut on his leg would end his young life, at the tender age of sixteen.

The liklihood of Hugh Tod owning the little cap gun is great. He was the only little boy living there at the time.

Dover 'Sad' Iron

"Mom, I need my best dress for church on Sunday. Will you please wash and iron it for me?", were probably the words which came from little ten year old Libby, many times, to her mother, Jessie. To Jesse, just the words were tiring. She would have to scrub the dress, thick and heavily laden with lace in a washtub, using home made lye soap and a scrub board. Then she would have to hang it on a clothesline, to drip and dry, weather permitting, or she would hang it inside to dry near the woodstove. Now, Jessie's work had just begun. She would spend the next hour or two ironing the dress first, with the regular heavy iron, which weighed from 5 to 7 pounds, and then she would finish the job by using the little 'sad' iron to press yards and yards of delicate lace, all completed without damaging the dress. The end result——a very pretty little girl.

There was certainly no shortage of petit little Robinson girls who grew up in Point Blank. There was Libby, Bess, Elizabeth (Pud), Marjorie, Bitsy, Dorothy, Ruby Lee, and Fannie Rose. All wore Victorian style dresses, adorned with lots of lace.

The little 2x4 boat-shaped iron that our daughter-in-law, Karla, dug up, was undoubtedly the one used by the Robinson girls. It is a Dover 'Sad' Iron, dated May, 1900, Canal Dover, USA.

1847 Rogers Bros. Silver Spoon

"Mommy won't mind. I'll take it back in the dining room when I'm through playing with it", thought Fannie. Fannie's mother, Mary Mcgowen, had come from the well-to-do McGowens who owned a large plantation at Camilla. Mary's mother certainly wanted her daughter to have only the finest silver ware available. The only daughter of Robert Tod Robinson, found herself having to create playtime activities of her own. After all, those five brothers of hers didn't want Fannie around playing the boys' games. So with sand bucket in one hand, and her mother, Mary's silver plated tablespoon in the other, she began to dig in the front yard, and play in a world of her own, building sand castles and dreams.

But Fannie forgot to return the beautiful spoon to her mother's dining room, so it sank into the ground, deeper and deeper into the dungeon of death. There it remained for 150 years, until my son, Vince, and grandson, John found it with the metal detector, ten inches down, where little Fannie may have left it, so many years ago. Today, it lives once again, on display in the museum for all to see.

Left to Right: Libby, Bess,and Marjorie Robinson
1925

Chapter 16

Interview With Thomas Earl
and Jeanne Walters

"I got one, I got one, Thomas Earl," I said excitedly, while rocking the boat. "Well, bring him in," shouted Tom. It was 1979, and the Principal of the school in Coldspring, Thomas Earl Walters had invited me to go fishing for catfish. He was also my neighbor, and the Mayor of Point Blank. The mighty Trinity had been dammed up in the late 1960s, creating Lake Livingston. We had motored out quite a distance from shore in Tom's bass boat, when he slowed down and appeared to be studying the shoreline. He was getting a cross between a house on one shore and a light pole on another shore. "Now, drop that rear anchor down right about there," he instructed. I wondered what in the world he was doing. We were in deep water. Suddenly, I heard a 'clink.' "What did the anchor hook onto?," I asked. Thomas Earl replied, "That's old Highway 190 down there. You hooked onto the bridge." Tom added, "I used to raise cattle here. Now, I raise catfish." I caught two fish that day, and Tom caught many more.

When September, 2010 came, I thought about Thomas Earl and his wife, Jeanne. They had a long history in Point Blank, especially Jean, whose maiden name was Butler. They knew the Robinsons very well. Barb and I paid them a visit one day, and asked them a few questions. Jeannes family, the Butlers, had bought part of the land in the late 1930s that had once belonged to the Robinsons, for $9.00 per acre.

"Tom, your land here, is where Tod, Sr.'s cotton gin was located, isn't it?" Tom replied, "Hold on, we have a photo." The picture was Jeanne and her uncle's brother, riding horses in front of the old gin. This was about a stone's throw from where we were sitting in the dining room. "I see a water tower in the background", I commented. Jeanne explained, " Yes, that's the water source they used to cool the engines down." The photo had been taken in 1949, when Jeanne was about 14 years old. "Tom, you tore down the gin, didn't you?", I asked. "Yes, and I used the lumber to build the house across the street, which our daughter, Nina Beth lives in," Tom explained.

There was another photo which showed a second water tower next to a shed. "That was our source of drinking water,"Jeanne explained. Tom added, "I helped build the shed that is there now. The reason we put a shed over it was because he (Jeannes father), had an electrical compressor, which pumped air into the well and forced water into that big tower. From the gravity feed, the water flowed down here into the house. Eventually, we added a pressure pump to it, and then had water pressure in the house.

Jeanne and Thomas Earl Walters
2010

In discussing the Big House, the one that Tod, Sr. had built across the highway from the plantation house, Tom and Jeanne explained that it had been there until the lake began to rise in the 1970s. The developers who had bought the Governor's Point subdivision, tore it down. It had been unused, except for renters, and was in much disrepair. It was a home which had represented the golden age of the plantation, but had died along with much of the memories of the Robinsons. Barbara asked Jeanne, "Was anyone living in the big house when you were little?" Jeanne replied, "Oh, yes! Grandma Robinson was, Mrs. Ora Lee (Tod, Sr.'s wife)."

Jeanne Walters Butler, 14
Riding 'Missy' in front of the cotton gin. 1949

"When you were a little girl, Jeanne, who was living in the plantation house?,"I asked. "Libby, and her mother and daddy was. Later, Libby's mother went to Houston to work at Foley's Department Store. Libby married R C Hansen, and when he retired, they moved back into the plantation house with Ms Jesse, Libby's mom. That was in the 1950s. Her dad, Aubrey Hugh, had passed in 1945."

I then asked Tom and Jeanne if either of them recalled the Robinsons making a trip to South America. They answered, 'No.' The reason I asked was because Barb and I had found a coin the day before in front of the house when Barb was planting her oak trees. It was a silver coin from Guatemala, dated 1945. We were thinking that maybe Libby and her husband had taken a vacation to Guatemala.

Barb commented, "The main thing I found yesterday, while digging a hole for my tree was a little pistol. Usually, Bill finds artifacts while looking for them, but I usually find them accidentally. I looked right in my shovel, and there it was. I said, Bill, either I have found a gun, or a water faucet. It was too coroded to tell. " I handed Tom the gun and asked, "What do you think, is it a toy, or is it real?" He looked it over, and said, "That would be a toy." "How do you know," I asked. Tom explained, "I have one very similar to it that I found awhile back. It's weight and the fact that it appears to be solid cast iron, makes it a toy." I replied to Tom that I had to be careful when finding artifacts. I have to be sure to call an artifact what it really is, rather than what I want it to be.

Tom added, "Talking about digging up iron, you could go right here at the end of our barn and find all kinds of iron metal. That's where the blacksmith's shop was." "Yes', I answered, I remember reading about the blacksmith's shop. I think one Isaac Owens worked there for the Robinsons." Jeanne interjected, "Yes, I knew Mr. Isaac, and his wife, but he had a shop of his own down toward the river. This shop was not his."

Barb commented, "Evidently, there was still a lot of cotton grown when you were small, Jeanne." Jeanne explained, "Well, there was pasture, and woods, and everything, but when you got down close to the river, that's where they grew the cotton. At that time everybody had their own little farm, so you would see patches of cotton here and there. Daddy grew a lot of cotton down there. There was also a man named John Trushell who bought land down by the river, but he and his family raised cattle, not cotton." Thomas Earl added, "Mr. Butler used to own the part that John Trushell had. What they would do is go in and buy a tract of land, clean it off, and plant cotton, and they would keep planting cotton until the land became depleted for cotton. Then, they would sell that tract, and go buy another."

Barb asked, "Was there a big drop off to the river bottom land, or was it gradual?" Tom explained, " It was more rolling and gradual. There was a first bank, and then a second bank, and then the river. In fact, those trees that are out in the middle of the lake, they were on the second bank, and the lake developers couldn't get to them with their bulldozers, so they were just left standing there. Good fishing place!" Jeanne added, "When the river would rise and go back down, prehistoric bones would come to the surface. My Daddy found a large dinosaur tooth, and part of a dinosaur backbone vertebrae. He put them in a museum in Livingston.

First Black Co-ed at Rice University

At this point, Thomas Earl and Jeanne showed us something extraordinary. They had a <u>Houston Post,</u> Sunday newspaper magazine, which featured on the front page, the young black girl that Bill and Bess Blythe had mentioned as having been the first African-American coed to attend Rice University in Houston. It was dated, September 12, 1965. Her grandparents lived close to the creek on the Robinson plantation. The article read:

> Rice's First Negro Co-ed--When Jacqueline McCauley was 4, she and her family drove past Rice Institute. Upon learning it was a college, she announced, "That's the college I'm going to when I am 8." It has taken her a little longer than she figured----10 years to be exact---but her prediction has come true. She graduated from Kashmere Gardens High School in June and starts classes at Rice this fall.

Jackie turned down substantial scholarships from three other schools to go to Rice. Last spring she became the first Texas negro to win a National Merit Scholarship and received personal letters of commendation from Congress and the White House. She worked this summer on NASA's flight to the moon project. And now she has become the first Negro girl and one of the first two Negro undergraduates admitted to the Rice University...

First 'Federal' Post Office Building in Point Blank

Another 'first' we discovered at the Walters' home, was a photo of the very first U. S. Post Office in Point Blank. The photo was taken in 1938, and had Jeannes cousin, Phil Thomas, standing in the doorway. It was the first official post office, even though Tod Robinson had been Postmaster as early as 1884. If this first Point Blank post office had a pungent odor to it , it is because this new post office had actually been a chicken coop. Yes, a chicken coop. But with full recognition, Jeannes mother received an official letter from Price Daniel, 38th Governor of the state of Texas, dated August 1, 1975.

RICE'S
FIRST
NEGRO
CO-ED

WHEN
Cau
her famil
Institute.
was a c
nounced,
I'm goin
It has
longer t
years t
predicti
She g
mere (

in June and starts classes at Rice this
Jackie turned down substantial scl
other schools to go to Rice. Last s
first Texas Negro to win a National
received personal letters of commer
and the White House. She worked t
flight-to-the-moon project. And no
first Negro girl and one of the firsl
uates admitted to the Rice Universit
Edward Freeman III of Port Arthur.

, Jacqueline McCauley is one of the first

Jacqueline McCauley
1965

Mrs. W. W. Butler
P. O. Box 34
Point Blank, Texas 77364

Dear Mrs. Butler:
Thanks for your letter of July 28 and the enclosed picture of
the Point Blank "Federal Building" in 1938. This was very
interesting, and if you can send me some details about the
building and it's Post Master, I will appreciate same. In the
meantime, as soon as I can get the picture copied, I will return
it too you.

Kindest personal regards,
Sincerely yours,

Price Daniel

P. S. Was this building used for a smokehouse, or some other purpose before it was designated as the Post Office?

Continuing our conversation, Barb asked Jeanne, "Do you remember where the outside kitchen was located next to our house? We were told that it was much like Sam Houston's place. That is, the kitchen was located outside of the dining area. The food was prepared outside and brought inside." Jeanne responded, "I remember there was a small log building straight out of the back of the house. That might have been it." Tom suggested, "That also could have been the smokehouse. Everybody had a smokehouse in those days." Barb agreed, "I'll bet Tom is right. It probably was their smokehouse. The old outdoor kitchen was probably gone by then." Tom remembered, "That reminds me of my Grandpa. He would often slip into the smokehouse with his long pocket knife, and slice some of that lean meat off the bacon, and boy, you talk about good. That was it."

First Official U.S. Post Office Building
Point Blank, TX 1938

We began a discussion about the possible location of the original draw well, which the slaves dug on the plantation. I suggested to Tom that we may have found it, but have not had time to dig and verify its location. When Barb was planting her oak trees, we found a water pipe which seemed to lead from the house to the area where we were told the well might be, or vice-versa. If it does lead from the well to the house, it could have been an artesian well, with water piped directly into the house. Tom grinned, and commented, ''Start diggin', and find out."

Barb, then asked Tom, ''Just exactly what is an artesian well, Tom?" Tom explained, ''Right down at the foot of the hill nearby, Mr. Bill (Jeanne's dad), had an artesian well. Here's a photo showing Mr. Bill standing beside the well, and next to a man who came to appraise the land for the Trinity River Authority. What they did was drill 212 feet, and hit a rock. They drilled through that rock, and then blew it with air, and that artesian well came up. It was full stream---lots of water. When we built our house across the road, they drilled down 407 feet, and the drill just dropped down. Water came up within 44 feet of the top of the ground, so there's a big underground resevoir there. And that was up on the hill. Down here, it came out. Do you remember Luther Hopkins? He's the one who built the 'Hop Stop' store up there where the Exxon station is now. They came in and drilled his well at 411 feet. When they drilled mine, it was 407 feet. He and I used to fish together, and he once said, laughingly, 'If I ever get mad at you, I'm gonna' turn my well on, and drain yours."

As Barb and I said goodbye to Thomas Earl and Jeanne, we thanked them for such wonderful hospitality, and for sharing so many stories and memories with us. I also quietly contemplated what great things the discovery of the artifacts had resulted in. In this case, friends were brought together to discuss and laugh about times past, and enjoy the good fellowship of the present.

Chapter 17

Billie Trapp—Educator, Historian

October 7, 2010

The history of San Jacinto County cannot be discussed or written about without mentioning the name of Billie Trapp. Through the efforts of this 80 year old legend of Coldspring, Texas, the lives of the pioneers of early Texas buried in this area will live on for generations to come. She is a former educator at Coldspring, second Chairman of the San Jacinto County Historical Commission, member of the Historical Commission today, and a long time friend , and relative-thru- marriage, of the Robinson family. She lives across the street from the courthouse (appropriate for historians), and is actively involved in the preservation of Old Town Coldspring. She allowed me one evening to come to her home and take a peek inside the brain of a walking history book.

Billie, I asked, "Weren't you the first chairman of the Historical Comission?" "No, I was the second, she answered. When the State Comission first came out, not many counties joined it. Eventually, all the counties joined. Their emphasis at that time was on the creation of historical markers. We're talking about the early 1960s. I was chairman for several years, and then resigned because I was starting college at the ripe old age of 36."

"Is that what led to the presentation of the historical marker at the Robinson Plantation in 1975?, "I asked. She answered, "Well, we just encouraged people like the Robinsons who might have a historical site to apply for a marker. But there were different kinds of markers. For example, the Subject marker: The Methodist Church right here in the next block close to where I live could have been on the National Register of Historical Sites, except for the fact that it had been moved from it's original location.

Grandaughter
Laura Rose Whitley West
At the historial marker
2010

San Jacinto County Courthouse
as seen from Billie Trapp's Balcony
2010

There was a lady by the name of Lucy McMurrey, who was my history mentor, that in the early1930s was appointed by the County to select four historical sites in San Jacinto County, to help celebrate the Texas centennial of independence from Mexico (1836-1936. I think she was probably the District Clerk at that time. The state had instructed her to locate these sites, and they would put a historical marker there. Let me see if I can remember them. One was at Raven Hill. Another one is between Coldspring and Camilla toward the lake, off of Farm Road 1514, and it's where Sam Houston's brother-in-law lived, Margaret Lea's brother. This is supposedly the meeting site where Sam Houston would counsel with the Alabama- Coushatta Indians. It's on private property today, owned by the McMurreys. There were two Indian villages in the county. One was at Point Blank, and one at the farthest end of San Jacinto County. The one at Point Blank was at Darby Hill. The chief was Ben Ash. In fact, Governor Wood's daughter, Mary, later put her return address as 'Ben Ash Hill'. I have some letters that she wrote. The Indians tribal grounds are under water now.

129

Well, getting back to the historical marking system, Miss Lucy was appointed by the county because she was an older woman and really knew a lot of its history. The markers were at Raven Hill, Council Hill (where Sam Houston met with the Indians), Swartout, which was a major crossing on the Trinity River, and for the life of me, I can't remember the fourth. Anyway, the point is that these four markers were not highly researched. But years later when the Historical Commission was initiated, probably in the late 1950s, requirements for a marker became much more strict. They were really smart the way they started it. They wanted a lot of things, but especially proof. They didn't just take your word for it, but they wanted documentation for the information you were giving them."

'OK, then, Billie', I asked, 'what led up to the state presenting the historical marker to the Robinson plantation?" Billie responded, "They just had pride in the place, as we did for the McClanahan marker at our place. They had not only a lot of pride in the plantation, but in the family, especially Bess Robinson and the Blythes. Bill was a State Representative at that time, so he was instrumental in getting the history and documentation together, to be submitted. I'm sure if you never got what they submitted, you could write to the state and get it. Write to the State Historical Commission, and ask how you can pull that up.

The procedure followed for getting a marker was that you submit all you know about the history of your property---names, photos, the ones that came first, and the building of the house, dates, and marriages. Then, the State looks through all of this, and they come up with the wording. They send a copy to the relatives, or persons responsible, who in turn makes suggestions, or changes. The State then rewords the marker, and makes it final.

Changing the subject, I asked, "Ora Lee McClanahan Robinson, a relative of yours?" Billie answered, "Yes, That's my husband's family. When the McClanahans first came to Texas, they settled in Point Blank. That would be in the 1850s when they came, so they would have known the Robinsons anyway. Later, they moved to Coldspring. In fact, the McClanahans and the Robinsons were in business together in Old Town Coldspring."

Letters From Mary D.

When asking Billie if she had any good stories from the past, she commented that she had a few, but a person better than her for good stories was Mary D. Robinson. Billie said, "Mary D. could write as though she were talking to you. You could just visualize everything she wrote. Billie had a couple of letters from Mary D. dated 1962, and 1963 when Mary was 68 years old. Billie had written to her inquiring about the history of San Jacinto County. She pulled the letters from a file cabinet next to a stately looking wooden desk. She said the desk had belonged to the Honorable Cornelius Ware Robinson, and had been handed down to her. So I read the letter dated September 13, 1962, and here are a few excerpts from Mary D.'s lengthy letter:

My dear Billie,
Please forgive me for not replying to your letter at an earlier date, but have been in bed for two weeks—just another heart flair up...
'Get out or I'll shoot!'
John Cunningham's uncle, (I can't remember his name), lived alone up in the woods above the Cunningham place in a one room log house surrounded by a tall rail fence. If anyone rode up to the rail fence, he poked a double-barreled shotgun out of a crack in the logs, and ordered them to leave. Mrs. Jones had told me about him. He had cancer of the nose, and it was eating his face up. Said he kept wet Bull Durham cigarette papers on his face and nose. That excited my curiosity, so one day I saddled my horse, loaded my saddle bags with food and preserves, and my pants pockets with Bull Durham cigarette papers, and rode five miles to see him. Seems as if I talked for hours before he ever put the shotgun down. I had tied my horse and climbed the rail fence, with him telling me to 'Get out or I'll shoot!' I got half-way from the fence to the door before he put his gun down. I went to the door and handed him the cigarette papers, and he said, 'Sit down. I'll be out in a minute.' So I sat on a log, and later, after he put wet papers on his face, he came out. We became good friends, and I often rode up to see him.

As I read this letter, I became increasingly amazed at the similarity between this story, which happened around 1920, and the modern day song *Joshua*. In the song the young girl pays a visit, out of curiosity, to a big, mean, man who lived all alone in a run down shack, and wouldn't let anyone come around. The young lady befriends the man, Joshua, and ends up marrying him. Of course, the real story, and the song, part ways in how each story ends.

A few days after I read this letter, I wondered whether I might be successful in finding out the name of this poor man whom Mary D. had befriended. My research into local history had been fun and partly successful, but this would be a challenge. Billie had mentioned that the Cunninghams once lived up on FM 946 by Willow Springs. I didn't know the Cunninghams, but I did know the Hillhouses' who lived up there. So I called my old friend, Craig Hillhouse and asked him about the Cunnninghams. He couldn't tell me much, but suggested I call another long time resident, Kenneth Street. Kenneth knew nothing of the character in the story, but thought that the Hillhouses and the Cunninghams were related, and suggested I call another long time resident who lived nearby, by the name of Floyd Hillhouse. So, I called Floyd, told him the story, and he knew just exactly who the cancer stricken man was. "That would be 'Bob Parks', Floyd said. 'He was suffering from cancer of the nose. He was related to my family, and I can show you exactly where he is buried."

I was ecstatic. I had matched a name to a letter written in 1962, that a woman who was born in 1895 couldn't remember. The next day, I met Floyd at his house close to Willow Springs. He invited me in, where I met his lovely wife, Beverly. The three of us talked about local history for nearly an hour.

Floyd suggested we needed to go find Bob Parks grave soon, before it was too dark. So we drove on a dirt road way back in the deep, deep piney woods. There was nothing but thick woods, a narrow dirt road, and a rattlesnake crossing the road. After several miles, Floyd slowed down, looked carefully at the side of the road, and said "I think this is it." After searching in the woods for a few minutes, Floyd said, "Here it is."

It was a solitary, lonely grave, marked only with a blank headstone and a footstone. I asked Floyd, "How do you know this is Bob Parks, since there is no writing?" He answered, "Because he is family."

As we walked back to our vehicles, I asked Floyd, "Where does this road lead?" He answered, "To your house. It comes out right at the back of your property."

I found it hard to believe. I didn't know of any such road. But trusting Floyd, I followed the narrow dirt road for about three miles when I came to an old wooded bridge. As I crossed the bridge, I recognized the road. It was Wilderness Road, leading right up to the back of our house. This road had always been closed just beyond the bridge because it was on private land, but now it was open.

Now, I understood better what had taken place here in the early 1900s. Mary D. had saddled up her horse at the house, filled her saddle bags with food and Bull Durham papers, and rode up this little dirt road, or trail, to visit her shotgun totin' friend, Bob Parks, many times.

MaryD.s letter continued:

The Grey Goose'

Aunt Ora McClanahan, Uncle Tod's wife, was born on Palmetto Creek before Grandpa McClanahan moved to Coldsprings to work in the Robinson & McMurrey store and saloon. Grandpa McClanahan told me this: There were three saloons in Point Blank precinct when I (Mary D.) came there---The 'Blue Goose' on Palmetto Creek, owned by Ben Johnson, the 'Grey Goose' where Kickapoo Creek ran into the Trinity River, operated by Uncle Harry Robinson, and the 'Goose' at Point Blank, owned by Uncle Tod, and operated by Charlie Groom and Arnett Jones, Sr.. The Goose stayed open only on Saturdays. I have one of the tokens used. You paid the money at the store, and got a token to spend at the saloon.

I have seen several killings on Saturdays back of the saloon, from my front porch. I was at the Grey Goose sitting on the bar when Tom Sprott walked up to Uncle Harry at the side door with a .45 revolver in his hand. Uncle Harry had a jigger of whiskey in his right hand, and his left hand was on the door facing-----A shot rang out, and Tom Sprott fell dead. Uncle Harry hadn't moved... Indian Jim killed Tom Sprott with Uncle Harry's 30-30 Winchester that I now have. He saw Sprott draw on Uncle Harry, and fired from a tree on the river bank. Yet, Uncle Harry always claimed that he had killed Tom Sprott. Believe me, those were wild and wooly times when I came to San Jacinto County in 1910...

The Lonely Grave of Bob Parks
2010

Swartout

Swartout was on the Trinity River below Camilla. Aaron Burr sent Colonel Swartout with a large number of troops and settlers by boat to this crossing on the river. Aaron Burr planned to join Colonel Swartout with more troops and take over the Southwest from Mexico. But after Burr's duel with **Alexander Hamilton**, in which Hamilton was killed, Burr's backers in this scheme deserted him and Burr took refuge on an island in the Mississippi called Blennerhassett. Colonel Swartout and some of the men returned to the East, but others went on West. Colonel Swartout's grandaughter, Gladys, was a famous opera singer years ago.

The Gindrats

The original Gindrats came from Demopolis, Alabama. Martha Gindratt, a widow with three children, married Governor Wood. They had several children of their own. Also, Florence

Dissosway was brought from Demopolis by my Grandfather, Robert Tod Robinson as a teacher or Governess for his children. She eventually married a son of Colonel Wheeler. All the people that founded the town of Demopolis, Alabama were from France, sent over there by **Napoleon Bonaparte** to be a unit of French colonization in the new world...

Point Blank Stores

The old Bob Robinson store was used by Uncle Willie, and Uncle Harry Robinson, but was destroyed by fire. They dissolved their partnership, and Uncle Harry built a building across the road that was the building Uncle Tod fixed up for me to use when I opened a store at Point Blank, and became Post Master. Uncle Tod built the two-story red building that his store was in. I have a picture of Uncle Tod sitting on the front porch of his store, but it doesn't show any part of the store, except the porch.

Governor Wood and Chief 'Ben Ash'

Governor Wood lived in a four room log house at Ben Ash Hill (Darby Hill) . A 'dog trot' ran through the house, two rooms on each side, really just a wide open hall. The kitchen was in the back yard, and Governor Wood's mother lived in a one room log house in the front yard, and died there. This information was given to me by my grandmother, who rode a mule with a side saddle when Governor Wood sent for her...

The Ben Ash Hill place was purchased from Governor Wood by Uncle Willie Robinson. The Point Blank place (Woods home), was built by my Grandfather's brother, Henry Robinson. Henry sold it to Governor Wood. I think this land was bought from Colonel Wheeler. I know the old Bob Robinson place (land), and the house that Libby lives in was built by Bob Robinson just before he married Mary McGowen of Camilla, who was his first wife. My Grandmother, Bob's second wife, was Virginia Eldridge Haden, of Columbus, Mississippi.

Chief Ben Ash, was chief of the Alabama-Coushatta Indian tribe, and camped out on a hill across the Trinity River at what was known as Indian Hill, or Kickapoo Creek, in Polk County. Years later, Uncle Lee Robinson bought some of that land and built a house on it...

Years ago, I was invited to a Congressional hearing concerning the Presbyterian Church on the Alabama-Coushatta Indian Reservation. I met a Coushatta Indian from Louisana, who testified before the committee, and said his name was John Robinson. After his testimony, I got up and followed him out the door, and questioned him. He told me his Indian name, and he said they used to cross the Trinity River, and camped under a hill at a spring. He said they traded venison, and skins with a man named Bob Robinson, who only had one arm. Bob told him his name was too long, so he would just call him John, and John said that he, John, added the name Robinson. This Indian was 98 years old when I talked to him. The spring was just below the cemetery at Point Blank. My Grandmother told me of the Indians camping there...

A Tribute to Billie

I do think you deserve credit in writing a history of San Jacinto County, I do hope I live long enough to read it. I spent a day in 1929 in Dallas with Governor Wood's daughter, Mrs. Aubrey, at her daughter's home in Oak Cliff. She told me many interesting things, among them, one about Governor Wood riding a mule, Old Pantalette, to Austin when he was Governor...

Best regards,
Mary D."

Harry, Ora Lee, and Tod, Sr.

In Mary D.'s letter to her sister, Polly, dated January 19, 1963, she asked Polly to relay information concerning how the Robinsons and McClanahans came to be related:

Tell Billie, Aunt Ora graduated from Coldspring High School a year before she married Uncle Tod. A year before that, Uncle Harry Robinson finished at Coldspring, then went to college at Moscow, Texas. He and Aunt Ora were engaged while at Coldspring High. It was broken off when Uncle Tod's wife, Lizzie Henry died. Aunt Minnie, Uncle Yancy's wife, told Uncle Tod about her sister, Ora. Uncle Tod told me that he

went to see Ora one time, and asked Bob McClanahan for her hand. On the next trip, they were married...
Do not know when I will get this mailed. It is zero degrees in Dallas. Better be glad you are not here.
Love to you,
Mary D.

Billie and I continued with our discussion: "Billie you've always been involved in the history of San Jacinto County. What did you enjoy doing the most in relation to it's history," I asked. She answered," Just simply recording it, I suppose, and just being a part of it." With a big smile and a giggle, Billie commented, "No one ever shares your enthusiasm for things. In fact, they get kind of bored with you talking about it so much. My son, Robert Trapp, is good enough to put up with it. I was always fortunate enough to be able to have time to research history. When my son was first in Office, and sworn in as County Attorney in Coldspring, he was asked to say a few words. It was so funny the way he said he knew all about the county, 'I know this county very well because when I was a little boy, my mother drug me all over the county. I don't know how many attics she had me climb into just to see what was there.'

Billie continued, 'The most fun I had was when I had the time to roam, and didn't have to work. I was always going out in the woods alone, checking out old cemeteries, and grave stones. My husband, warning me about going out alone, said that one day they were going to find me in the woods shot to death, and that I needed to stop doing it. Well, I didn't stop it, but I went when he didn't know, and I was always home when my children got home from school. I had a lot of experiences when looking for cemeteries, before it became the popular thing to do.

There is a cemetery out in the deep, dark woods, out from Evergreen, that is the Youngblood family cemetery. I have interviewed lots of older members of families, before it became the popular thing to do. I didn't have a tape recorder, so I did the only smart thing I knew how to do-------make notes, and then write it out when I got home. That's the best I could do.

'A Bear in the Woods?'

There was this lady who told me about being good friends with a young girl from a family who lived near the Youngblood cemetery. The young girl had a grandmother who was old and senile, and that the young girl used to spend the night with her. The grandmother would just sit on the front porch and rock in her rocking chair. She knew just which board to rock on to make the front door open. Every evening, the grandmother would have the grandaughter take a pan of water and a clean towel, and set it on the grave of her favorite grandson who had been killed by a bear. Each night the grandmother made sure fresh water and a clean towel was set on the grave, supposedly so he could wash up and stay clean.

Well, I needed to see the epitaph on the grave, maybe to see if for sure he was killed by a bear. It took me a long time to find out where that grave might be, but finally the day came. I borrowed my father-in-law's pickup truck. It was an old heavy thing, with a cumbersome stick shift. The only living being that knew where I was, was the person who worked at the store in Evergreen. I stopped there, bought a coke, and made sure of the directions of where I was going. So I turned on 945 toward Cleveland, and soon turned again into the woods. I had to get out and open several wire gaps to get deeper into the woods, and then---there was the cemetery. It had an old wooden gate, leaning inward. I thought, 'I can just climb that gate.' I was so excited. I always carried a basket with me, for small items such as paper, pencils, and cameras. So with the basket in hand, I attempted to climb the locked wooden gate. When I jumped to the other side, I landed in a gopher hole, and twisted my ankle severly. I couldn't move. I was in such horrible pain. I looked at my ankle, and there was a great big knot on it. I was petrified! Now, I was faced with having to crawl back over the fence, and through those gaps. Of course, it was my left ankle, the one I needed to shift the clutch with. I had to literally make myself drive that old truck about ten miles back home. Anyway, I made it home and went straight to bed, but my ankle got bigger and bigger. It so happened that in our grocery store, which was downstairs from where we are now, we had a place for general feed for the farmers and ranchers. There was a big rat in the feed, so when my husband got home, he grabbed the shotgun to kill the rat. But when he passed by the children, they wanted to know what he was doing. So he teased them saying, 'You know what we have to do when a horse breaks his leg-----now we're going to have to shoot Mama.' The kids didn't think that was very funny at all. Anyway, as it turned out, I stayed in a cast for six weeks. I had ruptured a ligament in my ankle." I asked Billie whether she ever went back to the cemetery to find the boy's grave. She said she didn't, but when she checked the cemetery records, she discovered the little boy was not killed by a bear at all. The epitaph read, that he was killed by an "unexpected discharge of a gun."

Importance of A State **Archeological** Landmark

"You are presently a member, once again, of the San Jacinto County Historical Commission, aren't you, Billie?" I asked. "Yes, I am," she answered.

"Why do you think it is important that the Robinson Plantation be designated as a State Archeological Landmark, which it is in the process of, as we speak," I asked. "Well, I think the place is not unique in the county, as far as having slaves, and the original building and land, which is where you are finding the artifacts, but the fact that not many have pursued it's history as you have, and the fact that the home has been wonderfully preserved, and now you are finding many artifacts, will make it a special place as a Landmark." I mentioned to her that the Blythe family had researched, and knew a great deal more than I concerning the Robinson history. It has only been through the discovery of the artifacts that I have been inspired to bring to life once again the memory of the historic name of 'Robinson'.

What a priviledge it was for me to be able sit down with a lady of such class and humility, and to listen and record a little of the vast knowledge and expertise in the history of San Jacinto County that she posesses. She has made her mark, and the county will always quote the writings and words of Billie Trapp.

Chapter 18

Becoming A State Archeological Landmark

October, 2010

October, 2010 has emerged as the beginning of a possible historic conclusion to the reality of a State Archeological Landmark. In a few days, Barb and I will attend a meeting of the Texas Historical Commission in Kingsville, Texas, where voting on the nomination of the Robinson Homeplace as a State Archeological Landmark (SAL), will take place. How appropriate the timing, as October is Archeology Month.

On October 5th, we received in the mail a notice from the Texas Historical Commission in Austin. It read:

Re: *Nomination for State Archeological Landmark Status.*
Robinson Homesite—41SJ223
San Jacinto County

Dear Mr. And Mrs. West:

The Texas Historical Commission will consider nomination for the above referenced properties to be considered for designation as a State Archeological Landmarks under the Antiquities Code of Texas.

Our staff will present the nomination of the above properties to the Commissioners at the Texas Historical Commission Quarterly meeting currently scheduled for October 22, 2010. This meeting will be held in Kingsville, Texas at the Caesar Kleberg Wildlife Research Institute, Pinnell Auditorium, 1730 W. Corral Avenue, starting at 8:30 a.m. The property will also be discussed at the Antiquities Advisory Board meeting also in Kingsville on October 21, starting at 1:00 p. m., same location.

Thank you for your efforts to preserve the irreplacable heritage of Texas...

Sincerely,

Mark Wolfe
Executive Dirctor

Although it wasn't necessary, Barb and I wanted very much to attend this meeting. To us, it would be a momentous occasion. It would bring to fruition the importance of the discovery of close to two hundred artifacts, and would establish a connection with the State to preserve the plantation for all to enjoy, and to learn from. So, at 5am on October 21ˢᵗ, Barb and I began our six-hour drive to Kingsville.

The meeting was to be held in the Pinnell Auditorium, at the Caesar Kleberg Wildlife Research Institute, not far from the entrance to the famed and historic **King Ranch**. This was exciting! The meeting was scheduled for 1:00pm. We seated ourselves at the back, with three minutes to spare. There were about 14 board members sitting at a long table in front of the audience. A gentleman approached us, and handed us a copy of the agenda. In part, it read:

Texas Historical Commission
Agenda
Antiquities Advisory Board Meeting #59
And Archeology committee

This meeting of the Antiquities Advisory Board and Archeology Committee have been properly posted with the Secretary of State's Office according to the provisions of the Texas Open Meetings Act, Chapter 351, Texas Government Code. The members may discuss and/or take action on any of the items listed in the agenda.

Site of landmark nomination
October, 2010

1. Call to Order—Chairman Crain
2. Approval of Minutes—Antiquities Advisory BoardMeeting #58 minutes from July 29, 2010 (Austin, Texas)--Chairman Crain
3. State Archeological Landmark nomination information—Bruseth
   a. 41NU14/Oso Lake Midden, Nueces County, owned by the City of Corpus Christi
   b. 41GM78/Spa and 41GM63/Cabin sites, Grimes County, co-owned by Lillian and Evelyn Ramey (private landowners)
   c. *Robinson Homesite*, 41SJ223, San Jacinto County, owned by Bill and Barbara West (private landowners)

When they began discussion of the Robinson Homeplace, they asked whether I would like to speak on behalf of the Plantation. I was hoping for this moment. I smiled, and asked, "How much time do I have?" I thanked them for this opportunity, introduced my lovely wife of 51 years, and was delighted to speak. Trying to keep it to a minimum, I enjoyed sharing with them the setting on the Trinity River for the Plantation, it's history, and the discoveries we had made.

The Board Members were very receptive, and asked several questions. It was shortly thereafter that a vote was taken for the nomination of the Robinson Homesite. The voting was unanimous in favor of the nomination. One member, Ms. Bratten Thomason, who is the *Director of History Programs Division,* even suggested that we contact her if we were interested in nominating the Robinson Homeplace to the *National Register of Historic Places.* I knew that I was in heavy company when , after the Robinson business, they began showing slides, and discussing the progress being made on the excavation of the La Belle, the 17th Century LaSalle ship, which sank off of Matagorda Bay in 1687.

For me, the archeological events of the past year were no less than incredible, but it had also been a learning experience. Maturity in methods and procedures of skilled archeology would not come without mistakes. Enthusiasm should not exceed ones judgement. For example, children digging in an area where precious artifacts may be is probably not a good idea. Teaching them proper methods and procedures is far more important. Fortunately, little damage from mistakes of this kind had been done to the plantation acreage. Also, while metal detectors may be useful, they are not one of the primary tools of skilled archeologists. These professionals rely heavily upon magnatometry, research, detailed sifting of the soil, accurate documentation, and enough funds to do the job adequately. Funding by the state is the lifeblood for the continued professional archeology and preservation of historic sites across Texas.

On a breezy day in mid November, I walked up to the historic plantation house, sat on the steps, and laid back on the porch in the warm Texas sun, just as I had done on that first day 32 years ago. As I gazed up at the stately columns, my old friend seemed to smile with contentment. The answer had been 'yes' to all of my questions on that first day. We had raised our children here, and provided the same place for all eleven of our grandchildren. The West family shared many happy occasions here, such as family reunions, ball games, Christmases, Fourth of Julys, weddings, and we continue to this day.

For the Robinsons, their Texas birthplace has been preserved. Even without the discovery of the artifacts, the plantation home continues to be a symbol of pride in their family. But the amazing discovery of personal items , tools, weapons, etc., which were so much a part of the everyday life of generations past resulted in the startling re-creation of life on the plantation, as it really was. On January 28, 2011, the Texas Historical Comission in Austin officially approved the Robinson Homesite as a State Archeological Landmark. Through the dedication of part of the estate as a State Archeological Landmark, the opportunity now exists for future generations to share a part of early Texas history, which might otherwise have been forgotten, and thus enable the plantation to give and to live once again.

Resources

"A County Wide Chamber of Commerce," <u>East Texas</u> magazine. May, 1929, page 18.

Blalock, R. H. "A History of Point Blank." <u>San Jacinto-News Times,</u> 1975.

Blalock, R. H. "First Model T in San Jacinto County Recalled." <u>San Jacinto County: A Glimpse Into The Past.</u> Book III, 1994. Pages 19-20.

Blalock, R. H. "History of Snowtown." <u>San Jacinto County: A Glimpse Into The Past.</u> Volume II, pages 4-10.

Blalock, R. H. "Steamboats On The Trinity River." <u>San Jacinto County: A Glimpse Into the Past.</u> 1987, Volume I, pages 2-4.

Blythe Jr., Colonel William Jackson."Robinson Plantation, 1846." 1975.

"Congressman Speaks at Rotary." <u>Huntsville Item.</u> Thursday, June 18, 1931.

Cooper, Iva Jones. Family History: September 21, 2010.

Cutrer, Thomas. "Tod Robinson." <u>Handbook of Texas Online.</u>

"First Black Co-ed at Rice University." <u>Houston Post.</u> Sunday, September 12, 1965.

Johnson, Francis White and Winkler, Ernest William. "The Honorable Cornelius Ware Robinson." <u>A History of Texas and Texans</u>, Volume 4.

Polk, Jessie Mae Howard. Local History. August 15, 2010.

Robinson, Bess Tyson Blythe and Bill Blythe. Family History. August 2, 2010.

Robinson, Elizabeth (Libby) Hansen. Family History. July 28, 1995.

"Robinson, William, May 13, 1878." <u>Lowndes County Will Book C.</u> Pages 177-179.

<u>San Jacinto County Cemetery Records.</u> "The Tod Robinson Cemetery."

<u>Texas Teacher Daily Register</u>, Austin: State of Texas, 1921-22, pages 4-19.

Trapp, Billie. Local History. August 4, 2010.

Walters, Thomas Earl and Jeanne. Local History. August 10, 2010.

Williams, Amelia and Barber, E. C. <u>The Writings of Sam Houston, 1842.</u> Volume LV, pages 69-70.

<u>Texas Historical Commission Agenda</u>, Kingsville: State of Texas, October 21, 2010.

<u>Texas Historical Commission</u>, *Texas Statewide Preservation Plan, Case Study Number 1.* November 2, 2010.

CPSIA information can be obtained at www.ICGtesting.com
224299LV00001B/4/P